URBAN**GRAPE'S**
DRINK
progressively

URBAN**GRAPE'S**

DRINK
progressively

**From White to Red, Light- to Full-bodied,
A Bold New Way to Pair Wine with Food**

HADLEY & TJ DOUGLAS
Recipes by Gabriel Frasca
Foreword by Christopher Howell

SPRING HOUSE PRESS

Publisher: Paul McGahren
Editorial Director: Matthew Teague
Editor: Erin Byers Murray
Art Director: Lindsay Hess
Design and Layout: Jason Deller
Infographic Design: JSGD
Photography: Béatrice Peltre
Index: Jay Kreider

Spring House Press
3613 Brush Hill Court
Nashville, TN 37216
ISBN: 978-1-940611-58-7

Library of Congress Control Number: 2017944629

Printed in China

First Printing: November 2017

Note: The following list contains names used in *Drink Progressively* that may be registered with the United States Copyright Office: Alexana Winery; Alexander Valley; Atlantic; Badenhorst Family Wines (AA Badenhorst, Secateurs); Ballard County; Bandol; *Beverage Dynamics;* Blanc de Morgex; Bodegas Ateca; Bodegas Muga; *Bon Appetit;* BostInno; *Boston; Boston Common; Boston Home;* Boston Marathon; Cain Vineyard & Winery; Campari; Castelli di Jesi; Castello Romitorio; Castelveltrano olives; Château de Pibarnon; Châteauneuf-du-Pape; Claude Riffault; Cloudy Bay; Coca-Cola; Columbia Valley; *Cook's Illustrated;* Coravin; Corazon del Sol; Côte d'Or; Côte de Nuit; Couly-Dutheil; Dave Matthews Band; Domaine de Piaugier; Domaine J.A. Ferret; Dry Creek Valley; Dundee Hills; *Esquire;* Etna; EuroCave; E-ZPass; Facebook; Falanghina del Sannio; *Food & Wine;* Gil Family Estates; Google Earth; *Gourmet;* Graves; Greydon House; Gundlach Bundschu Winery; Honeycrisp apple; Instagram; Institute of Masters of Wine; Jolly Ranchers; Just a Taste; Kim Crawford; La Spinetta; Lail Vineyards; Lirac; Living; Louis Jadot; "Lover Lay Down"; Luca; MacGyver; Maldon's Salt; Marcona almonds; Marcel Lapierre; *Massachusetts Beverage Journal;* Microplane; Mouton Noir; Nantucket Looms; Paso Robles; Peay Vineyards; Per Se; Pessac-Léognan; Pouilly-Fuissé; Puligny-Montrachet; Racked; Rancho Gordo; Revana Winery; Rioja; Ruby Wines; Rutherford; Salice Salentino; Santa Maria Valley; *Saveur;* "She's My Cherry Pie"; Sideways; Smitten Kitchen; Solo; Sonoma; Starchefs.com; Stolpman Vineyards; Straight Wharf; Style Me Pretty; Swartland; Sweetgreen; TEDx; *Terroirist;* Tetra Pak; The Aquitaine Group; *The Boston Globe; The Boston Herald; The Daily Show; The Improper Bostonian; The New York Times; The Pour; The Silver Palate;* The Urban Grape; Twitter; *Tyler Florence's Ultimate Cookbook;* Ulacia; Ventuno; Vietti Winery; *Vineyard Harvest;* Vinho Verde; Wahluke Slope; Walla Walla; Warrant; Windows on the World; *Windows on the World Complete Wine Course; Wine Folly; Wine Spectator;* Wrangler; Yakima Valley; Yamhill-Carlton; *Yo Gabba Gabba!;* YouTube.

To learn more about Spring House Press books, or to find a retailer near you, email info@springhousepress.com or visit us at www.springhousepress.com.

FOREWORD

by Christopher Howell

WHAT WINE TO HAVE WITH DINNER tonight? How can we possibly find our way through the endless shelves of unreadable, indecipherable, humorous, witty, meaningless, and sometimes misleading labels? Today, our choices in wine are beyond bewildering. Wine comes to us from more than 60 countries the world over, and within each of them, countless regions. Then, there are literally thousands of varieties of wine grapes. To most, wine seems to be an impossible labyrinth. Dare to enter a wine shop or open a wine list, and you're not likely to get out unscathed. We need another way.

With their book, TJ and Hadley Douglas give us that way. Up on Spring Mountain, in the Cain Vineyard, vintage after vintage, while my small team and I have been tending the same vines, and each year harvesting a new wine, TJ has been buying and selling our wines (along with many others) and telling our story for more than fifteen years—in restaurants, in distribution, and now in his wine shop, The Urban Grape. Hadley does a marvelous job in articulating TJ's vision and in so doing, that vision has become theirs.

This book will show you how to make an easy choice of a great wine to pair with your meal, by drawing a path through the world of wine that cuts across regions, varieties, and vintages. By breaking their selection into simple categories, they give us a road map for our wine adventure, our voyage of discovery. TJ and Hadley make it fun.

But there is more to this trip. In my forty-year love affair with the vine, what I have learned is very basic: Wine is connected to the grapes, the vines, the soil, and ultimately to the vineyard where it grows. So, along your way through this book, look for a few themes. First, regions (exploring wine is like going on vacation): Think warmer and cooler regions, think cultures, think cuisines, think history, and think about the people who grew that wine. Next, consider complexity: Many wines, especially today, can be fruity, simple, and satisfying. Others can offer nuance and take you deeper, attracting your attention and holding your interest. Some wines transcend the boundaries of fruit, and take it to another level—these wines can be unforgettable.

I can think of no people better than TJ and Hadley Douglas to introduce you to the richly fascinating and satisfying world of wine.

Let the journey begin!

CHRISTOPHER HOWELL
Wine Grower, Cain Vineyard & Winery
Spring Mountain District, Napa Valley

CONTENTS

THE WHITES   22

THE REDS   120

PROLOGUE

IT SHOULD SURPRISE ABSOLUTELY NO one that TJ and I met in a bar on the biggest all-day drinking event in Massachusetts, the Boston Marathon. There are two options in Boston during the Marathon: You run in it, or you drink during it. I was drinking, and TJ, a bartender at the time, was serving those drinks. Our nascent relationship fermented in a pool of spicy Bloody Marys.

One of our first dates involved wandering around a wine store picking out bottles to drink in his back yard while we grilled. As our relationship deepened, wine was often involved. When we bought our first condo, we drank Champagne and ate pizza on the floor. He put as much thought into the wine we would drink the night of our engagement as he did into the ring itself. He researched the perfect wedding wine to make our guests' varied palates happy. After our children were born, I made family dinners and TJ paired the perfect bottle. A theme was emerging, and that theme was wine.

In May of 2008, TJ and I traveled to Italy for a week of eating, drinking, and touring. A few days into our trip, wine glass in hand, I asked TJ a question he seemed relaxed enough to answer: "So, what's your five-year plan looking like these days?" Without missing a beat, he answered by laying out the business plan for a still unnamed wine store. He was excited and I was intrigued.

The exhaustion of parenting two young children combined with the state of the American economy in 2008 pushed TJ's dreams to the back of our minds. But TJ didn't forget them, and eventually he started working on a financial plan for his fledgling business.

Despite everything on our plate, the wine store idea was blossoming and by late 2009 we had a name, The Urban Grape, a lease, and a whole lot of sleepless nights ahead of us. By early June 2010, we had done it: The Urban Grape opened its doors and within a year, we were named "Boston's Best Wine Store" by *Boston* magazine.

Wine continues to be a hallmark in our lives, whether we're trying a new bottle together, or exploring wine country side by side. People always ask us: How do you work together without driving each other nuts? Everyone seems to know someone who went into business with their spouse and ended up filing for divorce! And yet, the pressures of running this business together have never driven us apart. In fact, it's the opposite—as the years pass, we have complete confidence and trust in each other, in the good times and the bad. The fact that we take a moment each night to check in with each other over a good glass of wine certainly helps.

We always say that the mission of The Urban Grape is to help people make memories through the experience of wine. Wine has certainly been there for our most memorable moments, and our joy is making sure it's there for yours, too.

INTRODUCTION

WE'RE JUST GOING TO PUT THIS OUT there: We are not Masters of Wine. Most days, we—TJ and Hadley Douglas—are not masters of anything: our destiny, our kids, our to-do lists, and certainly not ever of our dog. But, there are 356 Masters of Wine in the world—men and women who have gone through extensive study and examination to demonstrate their wine knowledge to the Institute of Masters of Wine—and they've worked incredibly hard to earn that title. These driven and highly educated men and women will likely forget more about wine than we will ever know. A few Masters of Wine have even written books on the proper way to pair wine with food. Yes, you could have picked up one of their tomes—maybe you already own a few. But what you're about to dive into is a book that offers wine and food pairings dictated not by rules, but rather by the belief that nothing is more transcendent than a plate of food and a glass of wine that seem destined for one another.

Here's why you'll be glad you did: Just like you can't solve a problem like Maria, much less pin a wave upon the sand, we don't think you can really *ever* master wine. Well, maybe .00000004% of the earth's population can. But *we* (you guys, us, the rest of the planet) will probably never get there. And *that*, that right there, is the beauty of wine.

Wine refuses to be mastered. It's a living, breathing, ever evolving, frustrating, confusing, and finicky thing. As humans, we've tried to impose our rules onto wine for hundreds of years. (Just take a gander at some of the AOC regulations in France, if you ever want to see rule-driven rigidity.) Sometimes, the wine will pretend to be tame—we call these "perfect" vintages—but then it will go right back to doing whatever it wanted to do in the first place. Wine doesn't even taste the same from the first sip in your glass to your last. How can you master something that simply refuses to make sense?

If wine can't be mastered, and certainly never tamed, can it be understood? We think so. The journey to understanding wine, and to fitting it comfortably into our lives, is what prompted us to open The Urban Grape, our little neighborhood wine store in the South End of Boston. Since the day we opened in 2010, our approach to understanding wine has won us legions of happy and loyal customers. They appreciate that we greet them at the door and ask them two simple questions: "What do you like?" and "What are you doing with it?"

"What Do You Like?"

This is *your* wine. It doesn't matter if a reviewer gave it a high score—if you think it tastes bad, than it's no good! At The Urban Grape, we set out to learn your wine language by asking you to describe the wines you love. After that, if time allows, we like to try some wine with you to get a sense for what excites you. From there we send you to a section of the wine wall, on a progressive scale from lightest bodied to fullest bodied, and help pick out the perfect bottle for *you*.

"What Are You Doing With It?"

Are you picking up a bottle to share with friends over a few nibbles before you head out to dinner? Are you bringing it to your grandmother's house to drink with Sunday supper? Are you serving it at a celebratory dinner to congratulate your wife on her promotion? All of these scenarios require something different. Most importantly, if there is food involved, *what is the food*? This is what we really want to know. This is where the fun happens.

Wine—which we've just described as the master-less wild child of our world—is made whole by the addition of food. It blossoms and sings, while simultaneously yielding its strident ways to soften, relax, and give in. Try the wrong pairing and you've got Warrant's "She's My Cherry Pie." Find the right pairing and you've got Dave Matthew's "Lover Lay Down." Just ask chef Gabriel Frasca, who went through numerous wrong pairings to create the recipes for this book before discovering his perfect playlist. It's all about the pairing, baby.

In this book, we will give you our thoughts, opinions, and philosophies on what works for us in the vast and often confusing world of food and wine pairing. Oh, and let's just leave those "white wine goes with fish" and "red wine goes with meat" clichés right here at the door, shall we? We'll give you easy, and sometimes not-so-easy, pairing suggestions and explain why they work. Occasionally, we'll take everything you just learned and throw it on its head—because for every wine rule, there's a wine outlier. You'll find regions and varietals that typically fall into each category of the Progressive Scale, which you can take to your own hometown wine stores in order to help recreate the right pairing at home. Along the way, you'll learn about us, and our journey with wine from those very first sips to what we drank last night. You'll discover

new regions and varietals. You'll learn about some of the world's most exciting winemakers, and finally learn what all those confusing wine terms mean.

We can't promise that you'll master everything on this journey (we certainly haven't). But we do know that you will eat and drink very, very well.

A Note About Voice

This book is a collaboration in every way—except in who put pen to paper. Somewhere in our marriage, we discovered that I (Hadley) had a unique ability to translate how he (TJ) talks about wine into a language that people could understand. When TJ talks about wine, passion and knowledge explode in a wine-colored rainbow. It can get confusing, and frankly, a touch long winded. I take notes, think about how it makes sense to people that know less about wine (i.e. me), and then write what he's said in an approachable way. That's exactly what we did for this book. So while you're not reading TJ's writing, necessarily, you are being taught his ideas, which we think have revolutionized how wine is sold in a retail setting. The voice you're hearing really is his, translated through my keyboard . . . with my silly side comments added in for fun.

As for the recipes, the star dish in each chapter is from Gabriel, who you'll see has his own very unique voice. He didn't need any help translating his tasty ideas into something we could all understand! The less formal dinner and pairing ideas come straight from our family dinner table.

Let's get started!

Chef Gabriel Frasca, and Hadley and TJ Douglas inside The Urban Grape

WHAT DOES IT MEAN TO DRINK PROGRESSIVELY?

We developed The Urban Grape Progressive Scale, a unique way of organizing wine from light-bodied to full-bodied—rather than by varietal or region—as a way to help our customers find the perfect wine for their palate.

Ranging on a scale from 1 to 10, with 1 being the lightest-bodied wines and 10 being the fullest-bodied wines, the Progressive Scale not only makes it easy to pick the right bottle every time, it also helps demystify wine's many regional, varietal, and production complexities. It's easy to feel confident discovering new wines when you *Drink Progressively!*

What is the Progressive Scale?

Speaking the same language is important with wine. That doesn't mean that you have to smell red fruit or leather in a wine when we smell red fruit or leather, but it does mean that we agree on some basic parameters that make up the framework for this book. To do that, we need to travel to the top of the North Tower of the World Trade Center in New York City, to a restaurant that was destroyed on 9/11: Windows on the World.

From 1976 to 2001, a self-taught wine lover named Kevin Zraly ran the wine program at Windows on the World. During that amazing tenure, Kevin oversaw what was considered to be the most remarkable wine program in the United States, with innumerable bottles that lured serious wine drinkers from around the world. He also became a fantastic wine educator, and wrote a book that many people credit with helping them to demystify wine: *Windows on the World Complete Wine Course.* When TJ Douglas, a 20-something living in Boston, read that book, he got the wine bug in a major way.

In the years right after Windows on the World was destroyed, TJ was managing restaurants in Boston and fine-tuning any wine list he could get his hands on. He was trying to figure out how to train his staff quickly and efficiently on the best ways to sell wine at the table, and he found his answer in Kevin's book. In a 2011 profile, *Esquire* writer Cal Fussman noted that Kevin Zraly "knew how to shrink the complex to the simple—a good quality to have if you're going to introduce people to wine. For example, he'd point to the three major varieties of white wine—Sauvignon Blanc,

Riesling and Chardonnay—and ask you to visualize them as skim milk, whole milk, and cream. Before you'd even tasted the wines, you had an idea of where they stood from light to heavy. Then he did the same for reds. Pinot Noir: skim milk. Merlot: whole milk. Cabernet Sauvignon: heavy cream. With that information alone, you could go into a restaurant, order a thick sirloin, and know that it was wiser to muscle up to the steak with a hearty Cabernet Sauvignon than a willowy Riesling.

Skim milk, whole milk, heavy cream. The concept was revolutionary for TJ. He thought nothing could be easier. When TJ set up his restaurant wine list using Kevin's "progressive format," as it was called, his staff grew confident, his diners felt relaxed, and wine sales skyrocketed. Was there any reason we couldn't take this

experience and turn it horizontally onto a wine store wall? Just because no one had done it before didn't mean it couldn't be done, right? And, with that, The Urban Grape's progressive shelving concept was born.

At The Urban Grape, progressive shelving comes in the form of our revolutionary 1 to 10 Progressive Scale. One is the lightest bodied wine we carry, our "skim milk." Things progressively build in body to 5, our "whole milk." We cap everything off at 10, our "heavy cream." We do this twice: 1W to 10W for white wines, and 1R to 10R for red wines. In this book, we've replicated those sections and created food pairings to coincide with each. It's as simple as this: If you can grasp how to *Drink Progressively,* you can demystify food and wine pairings. And, in case you really want to look like a

It's easy to *Drink Progressively* once you learn the basics. It's all about the body of the wine, which can be easily compared to familiar drinks like skim milk, whole milk, heavy cream, lemonade, and hot chocolate

1 Lightest bodied, tart wines have a mouth-feel similar to that of skim milk.

2 Grown in cooler alpine & maritime climates, these wines are light-bodied and acidic.

3 Slightly warmer temperatures produce riper grapes, which add fruit and body.

4 Moderate techniques like neutral barrels, lees contact, and cement eggs add texture and body.

5 Medium-bodied wines have more structure and a mouth-feel similar to that of whole milk.

6 Warmer growing regions, fully ripened grapes and barrel-aging add to the wine's body.

7 Diurnal shifts (hot days & cool nights) produce wines with ample body and acidity.

8 Old World regions and winemaking techniques are replaced by a bolder New World palate.

9 Fully ripe grapes and lengthy oak aging combine for very full-bodied wines.

10 The fullest-bodied wines have a mouth-feel similar to that of heavy cream.

pro, this book will also help you understand why different varietals and regions make wines with different bodies, and how the same wine varietal can be manipulated into different bodies by using various production techniques.

The other important thing to keep in mind throughout the book is whether you would pair a dish with "lemonade" or "hot chocolate." This is another easy Kevin Zraly cheat that will help you characterize a dish by season, as well as where and when you are drinking it. Imagine sitting on a porch on a hot summer day—you would reach for lemonade over hot chocolate. The same goes for your wine. Wines at the beginning of the Progressive Scale have higher levels of natural acidity, with a fresher taste and a brighter finish. When you take a sip of a "lemonade" wine, the pores in your mouth spring open, the salivary glands kick into gear, and you are quite literally drooling in anticipation of your next sip. We'll teach you how to choose the perfect wine and then reward your primed senses with a dish that has fresh, bright flavors and bursts of acid.

As we move up the Progressive Scale, we find wines grown in areas that have warmer growing seasons, where winemaker techniques like malolactic fermentation, lees contact, and barrel aging all amp up the body, texture, and mouthfeel of the wine. Meanwhile, acidity levels start going down. This is the world of cozy fires, chilly nights and . . . hot chocolate! "Hot chocolate" wines are at the other end of the Progressive Scale, and while some of them need savory recipes to make them more approachable, other "hot chocolate" wines are a meal unto themselves. Recipes that complement and engage "hot chocolate" wines can be found in the corresponding chapters throughout this book.

Skim milk, whole milk, heavy cream. Lemonade and hot chocolate. Now we're speaking the same basic language, and we're ready to dive into the no-longer-intimidating world of food and wine pairing.

The Importance of Vintages

Wine is not Coke Classic—it shouldn't taste the same with every vintage. If it does, you know you're dealing with a winemaker who is manipulating the product to please a board of directors and sales projections, instead of letting the wine speak for itself.

Growing seasons, or vintages, are affected by everything from bud break to harvest: temperature, precipitation, frost, and even bugs. Winemaking is farming, first and foremost! It is important to pay attention to vintages because different years will put forth different characteristics. It makes wine more confusing, but also more fun, once you get the hang of it.

That said, in this book, we have not marked specific vintages for our "One to Try" wines, because the realities of publishing mean that the stores would already have new vintages in stock by the time this book hits the shelves. Instead, we chose wines that have consistent body from vintage to vintage, even if their nuances, like aromatics, might change. We hope you'll use these wines as your guide as you explore and develop your own palate. Before long, you'll be an expert at Drinking Progressively!

THE WHITES

1W

Hailing from the coolest alpine- and maritime-influenced regions of Europe, including Txacholi, Spain; Minho, Portugal; and Savoie, France, 1W wines are steel-fermented with no oak aging. They're remarkably light-bodied with a mouthfeel like skim milk, and have tart, lip-smacking acidity. Common varietals include Hondarrabi Zuri, Alvarinho/Albariño, and Jacquère. Pair these wines with light dishes that have bright acidity.

2W

2W wines are grown in cool alpine- and maritime-influenced European regions like Muscadet and Sancerre, France; Alto Adige, Italy; and U.S. regions like the Finger Lakes in New York. The wines are fermented in steel, but some see sur lie aging, and are light-bodied with bright acidity. Common varietals include Riesling, Melon de Bourgogne, Sauvignon Blanc, and Pinot Grigio. They pair beautifully with a wide variety of seafood dishes.

3W

Influenced by slightly warmer regions such as Tuscany and Campania, Italy; Alsace, France; Willamette Valley, Oregon; and Marlborough, New Zealand, 3W wines are primarily steel-fermented, with some aging in concrete or neutral-oak barrels. They resemble 1% milk, and show increased fruit and texture, and vibrant acidity. Popular varietals are Vernaccia, Falanghina, Riesling, Pinot Grigio/Gris, and Sauvignon Blanc. Spring vegetables and soft, mild cheeses are great pairing options.

4W

4W wines are from a mix of warm and cool climates, including Burgundy and Loire Valley, France; Tuscany, Italy; Columbia Valley, Washington; and Stajerska, Slovenia. Winemakers use techniques like sur lie and skin contact, and neutral-barrel or concrete-egg aging to enhance body, texture, and complexity. Varietals include Chardonnay, Chenin Blanc, Vermentino, Semillon, and Pinot Grigio. These wines pair well with light pasta dishes and take-out food.

5W

This section includes wines from a mix of cool and warm climates from the most famous regions in the world: Napa Valley, California; Burgundy, France; and Mosel Valley, Germany. The first influence of partial malolactic fermentation and minimal oak aging can be seen in this section, producing wines with softer texture, enhanced fruit, and refreshing acidity that resemble whole milk on the palate. Popular varietals like Sauvignon Blanc, Chardonnay, and Riesling pair well with spicy foods.

6W

Increased warmth and sunshine in regions like Rhône Valley and Burgundy, France; and Sicily, Italy, produce grapes that are then influenced by partial malolactic fermentation and/or oak aging. The resulting wines have a creamy texture and integrated acidity. Varietals include favorites like Grenache Blanc, Marsanne, Roussanne, Chardonnay, and lesser-known grapes, like Carricante and Catarratto. These are wonderful with lighter, creamy dishes.

7W

Warm and abundantly sunny Old and New World climates, like Rhône Valley and Alsace, France; Rioja, Spain; and Santa Barbara County and Sonoma County, California, produce grapes that see partial or full malolactic fermentation and a mix of oak-aging techniques. The wines have a body like half & half with ripe fruit flavors, and softer acidity. Common varietals include Grenache Blanc, Marsanne, Roussanne, Viognier, Viura, Chardonnay, and Gewürztraminer. These wines pair nicely with game meats and earthy vegetables.

8W

8W is comprised of warm climates with sunny days and cooler nights in regions like Russian River Valley and Carneros, California; Northern Rhône Valley, France; and Columbia Valley and Walla Walla, Washington. Wines see full malolactic fermentation and a variety of oak-aging techniques to impart body and creaminess to the wine. Varietals include Chardonnay, Marsanne, Roussanne, and Viognier. These wines are delicious with Thanksgiving flavors.

9W

New World regions like Napa Valley, Sonoma Valley, and Santa Lucia Highlands, California; Casablanca Valley, Chile; and Stellenbosch, South Africa see long stretches of warm to hot weather. The resulting wines go through full malolactic fermentation and new-oak aging, making them creamy and smooth. Varietals like Chardonnay, Marsanne, Roussanne, and Chenin Blanc are ideal pairings for lobster pizza or BLTs slathered in mayo.

10W

Valley floor regions like Napa Valley and Santa Maria Valley, California, see abundant sunshine and long, hot growing seasons. Full malolactic fermentation and substantial oak aging produce wines that are flavorful and full-bodied with a voluptuous, creamy texture that resembles heavy cream. The primary varietals are Chardonnay and Viognier, which easily pair with rich dishes like lobster, fettucine alfredo, and even steak.

THE REDS

1R

Cool-climate regions, like Willamette Valley, Oregon; and Burgundy and Jura, France, produce low-tannin grapes that see minimal maceration and mostly stainless-steel aging. With little-to-no oak aging, the wines resemble skim milk with abundant bright acidity. Famous food-friendly varietals include Pinot Noir, Gamay, and Trousseau. Pair these wines with salty charcuterie and light salads.

2R

Primarily grown in cool-climate regions like Sonoma Coast, California; Burgundy and Loire Valley, France; Willamette Valley, Oregon; and Piedmont, Italy, these wines have a short maceration time followed by primarily steel or cement fermentation. The wines are light-bodied, tart, and acidic. Varietals include Pinot Noir, Gamay, Barbera, and Dolcetto. Savory herbs and tomatoes pair wonderfully with these wines.

3R

Temperate Old and New World climates in regions such as Burgundy, France; Willamette Valley, Oregon; Anderson Valley and Russian River Valley, California; and Etna and Piedmont, Italy, encourage further ripening of grapes. Cooler climates rely on longer maceration and light barrel aging; warmer climates use cement or stainless steel. The wines resemble 1% milk and have juicy ripe fruit and vibrant acidity. Varietals include Pinot Noir, Nerello Mascalese, and Barbera. Pair these wines with grilled seafood, salty capers, and olives.

4R

4R sees a mix of cool and temperate climates, and alpine and maritime influence in regions like Piedmont, Italy; Carneros and Russian River Valley, California; Bordeaux, Loire Valley, and Rhône Valley, France. Production techniques depend on the grape and climate; a variety of maceration times are used, as are stainless-steel or oak aging. The wines resemble 2% milk, with ripe fruit, balanced acid, and subtle tannins. Varietals like Nebbiolo, Cabernet Franc, and Sangiovese pair well with cured meats and grilled vegetables.

5R

Temperate climates in regions like Tuscany and Sicily, Italy; Rhône Valley and Bordeaux, France; and Casablanca, Chile, see a range of warmth and sunshine. Grapes see longer maceration and are primarily aged in a combination of new- and used-oak barrels. The wines have structured tannins and a medium body like whole milk. Varietals such as Sangiovese, Nero D'Avola, Syrah, Cabernet Sauvignon, Merlot, Cabernet Franc, and Carmenere are cellar-worthy, and pair nicely with braised meats and earthy vegetables.

6R

6R is mostly made up of warmer-climate wines from regions such as Tuscany, Italy; Rioja, Spain; Bordeaux, Châteauneuf-du-Pape, and St. Joseph, France; and Douro Valley, Portugal. Longer periods of oak-aging techniques add structured wood tannins to the wine. Blends made from Grenache, Syrah, and Mourvèdre, as well as varietals like Sangiovese, Tempranillo,

Cabernet Sauvignon, and Touriga Nacional produce food- and palate-friendly wines that pair best with regional dishes from the same provenance.

7R

This section includes drier, sunnier climates in regions like Napa Valley and Sonoma County, California; Columbia Valley, Washington; Bandol, France; Ribera del Duero, Spain; and Mendoza, Argentina. These wines see longer maceration and barrel fermentation, and can be aged in new oak barrels. They are bold wines with ripe fruit and integrated tannins and a body like half & half. Varietals include Zinfandel, Cabernet Sauvignon, Merlot, Syrah, Mourvèdre, and Malbec. They pair with a variety of savory dishes, including braised meats.

8R

Regions like Toro, Spain; Napa Valley and Sonoma County, California; McClaren Vale, Australia; Languedoc-Roussillon, France; and Puglia, Italy, see warm, sunny days, dry conditions, and long growing seasons. These wines are aged for longer periods of time in mostly new-oak barrels and have abundant fruit, less acid, and overall smoother tannins. Common varietals include Tempranillo, Cabernet Sauvignon, Zinfandel, Syrah/Shiraz, Grenache, Mourvèdre, Carignan, and Negroamaro. Pair them with meat and potato dishes.

9R

9R is mostly comprised of New World climates like Napa Valley and Dry Creek Valley, California; Walla Walla, Washington; Barossa Valley, Australia; Campania and Veneto, Italy; and Mendoza, Argentina, which are warm to hot, and have arid growing conditions. The resulting wines are juicy, jammy, richly tannic, and full-bodied. Popular varietals include Cabernet Sauvignon, Petite Sirah, Zinfandel, Syrah/Shiraz, Aglianico, Corvina, and Merlot. The wines are best paired with thick, juicy steaks.

10R

Hot, sunny, and arid growing regions like Walla Walla, Washington; Barossa Valley, Australia; Napa Valley, California; and Veneto, Italy, are found in the 10R section. The wines are fermented and aged in new-oak barrels for maximum impact. These are the heaviest-bodied wines, with a thick and jammy mouthfeel resembling heavy cream. The wines are made from Syrah/Shiraz, Petite Sirah, Zinfandel, and Corvina. While they don't always need food, they do pair well with barbecue and umami flavors.

THE
WHITES

CHAPTER 1

THE PORCH POUNDERS

Close your eyes and take yourself back to the hot and languid summer days of your youth. When your mom needed to cool you down in a hurry, it wasn't chocolate milk she gave you—it was lemonade. For adults, there's both a chemical and emotional reason we still reach for the lightest-bodied, most brightly acidic wines during the summer months. They quench our thirst, but they also remind us of that summer break, when we spent our days roaming freely without a care in the world. Sure, the Porch Pounders taste great all year long, but warm weather is when they really shine.

THE LIGHTEST
AND THE BRIGHTEST

THE WINE WALL AT THE URBAN GRAPE begins with the lightest-bodied of the white wines. All stories have to begin somewhere, and the Progressive Scale begins with fresh-styled, young white wines that are grown in cooler climates, and have seen little to no winemaker influence after fermentation.

We'll learn in Chapter 2 that sun and warmth produce grapes with higher sugar levels. If warmth equals sugar, than that means cooler growing regions produce grapes with less sugar. Lower sugar levels in the grapes produce wines that have lower alcohol levels and more acidity. Remember, acidity

AT A GLANCE

climate	The coolest alpine- and maritime-influenced regions of Europe
regions	Txakoli, Spain; Minho, Portugal; Languedoc and Savoie, France; and Valle D'Aoste, Italy
varietals	Hondarrabi Zuri; Alvarinho/Albariño; Picpoul de Pinet; Jacquère; Prié Blanc
technique	Steel-fermented, no aging or oak influence
characteristics	Remarkably light-bodied with a mouthfeel like skim milk; tart, lip-smacking acidity
color	Straw-hued or pale green
ideal pairings	Oysters, shellfish, and white fish; ceviche; light dishes and salads that have bright acidity

in wine is mandatory. Without it, wine would taste flat and boring. But the 1W wines have a lip-smacking tartness that the winemakers don't even try to tame. These wines are adult lemonade in every sense.

Ethereally light-bodied wines typically do not take well to oak aging; therefore, the 1Ws are almost uniformly produced in stainless steel tanks. A lack of post-harvest manipulation means that these wines are picked, fermented, and bottled in just a few months' time. The winemaker's goal is to move them to the buying market quickly, because these light-bodied wines are best consumed when they're young and fresh. This is good news for the consumer: Less work and storage means 1Ws are almost universally more affordable than other wines. But buyer beware: If you see a bottle that is more than a vintage or two behind the last harvest, move on! These wines are not made for lengthy storage.

Almost none of the wines in the 1W section are produced in the United States, and as a result, many of the grape varietals and regions have names that are difficult to pronounce and remember. (Hondarabbi Zuri makes Txakoli, also spelled Chacoli, from the Getariako, got it?) There is an easy cheat for 1Ws, however. In general, they are almost ghostly pale, with light green or yellow hues, and on the palate they are

characterized more by acid than by fruit. If someone hands you a translucent wine that you would describe as zippy, chances are good you've got a 1W.

GEEKOUT:
WHAT IS FERMENTATION?

To understand why cooler climates make wines with less alcohol, we've got to dive right into fermentation. After harvest, the grapes are crushed and the juice is put into vats. Next comes yeast. Some winemakers rely on naturally occurring yeasts found on the skin of the grape, while others add a specific strain of yeast to the juice. Different yeasts can add different nuances to the wine, but their job is always the same: the yeast eats the sugar in the grape's juice and turns that sugar into alcohol, carbon dioxide, and sulfites. Warmth and sun produce riper grapes with more sugar, which means cooler climates produce grapes with less sugar. Therefore, cooler climates produce wines with less alcohol.

Here are a few fermentation points to remember as we move through the book. The dead yeast cells are called *lees*. Leaving the lees in the barrel during aging can influence the wine's flavor, as well as its body by making it fuller. Red wine fermentation differs from white in that, with white wines, the juice is immediately separated from the skins after the crush. Red wines are fermented with their skins, which add color, body, and other important elements. And we won't discuss it just yet, but secondary fermentation, also called malolactic fermentation, is an incredibly important process that adds body and flavor to wines.

Our Favorite Regions and Varietals

Thanks to a plethora of cooler wine growing regions and maritime influence, Europe dominates the 1W section at The Urban Grape, particularly the Spanish region of Txakoli (also sometimes written as Txakolina, Txacholi, or even Chacoli). But just because we're staying in Europe doesn't mean there isn't a wide variety of grape varietals and regions to explore. Here are some of our favorites.

FRANCE

REGIONS: Languedoc and Savoie
VARIETAL: Picpoul de Pinet, Jacquère

France may be famous for its red wines, but the country's white offerings are also expertly made, including those from the Languedoc and Savoie AOCs. Picpoul de Pinet has been grown in the Languedoc for centuries. Characterized by its clear green hues, delicate flavors, and lip-smacking acidity, the varietal has caught on in the U.S. as the popularity of light-bodied white wines has increased. The Rhône Alps of France are home to the Vin de Savoie AOC, also commonly written as Savoy. The lightest-bodied wines from this region are made with the Jacquère grape, and are known for having enough neutrality and acid to cut through the region's signature rich fondue. Both of these varietals pair well with food, but are also lovely on their own.

ITALY

REGION: Valle D'Aoste
VARIETAL: Prié Blanc

The award for most awesome wine region might go to the Alps-surrounded Vallee d'Aoste in Italy. The smallest region in the country, Vallee d'Aoste boasts some of the highest-elevation vineyards in Europe, in the sub-appellation of Blanc de Morgex. The fast-ripening white wine grape Prié Blanc thrives in wind-swept vineyards and is not bothered by the area's short growing season—which is often punctuated by watching out for avalanches while harvesting! These are wines you can drink all day long and never tire of. They take some seeking out, but you'll be rewarded for your effort.

PORTUGAL

REGION: Vinho Verde
VARIETALS: Alvarinho, Loureiro

Portugal is known for wines from the cool, wet region of Minho, a wine producing area inside the country's largest DOC, Vinho Verde. The name translates to "green wine;" however, the reference is about the age of the wine and not its color—the majority of Vinho Verde wines are meant to be consumed in their youth. Vinho Verde includes nine sub-regions, and is associated with zippy, low-alcohol whites that are almost always made using a blend of grapes such as Alvarinho, Loureiro, Trajadura, Arinto, and Avesso. Alvarinho (more recognizably called Albariño in Spain) is the most well-known varietal thanks to its floral and fruity profile, balanced alcohol, and easy-drinking reputation. These whites tend to include a subtle spritz as a result of the fermentation process.

WHAT TO EAT WITH
— 1W WINES —

Like a tall glass of lemonade on a scorching hot day, 1W wines are all about quenching your thirst. Their zesty, abundant acidity awakens your palate and keeps you reaching for another sip. Keep the food pairing light and simple, or risk overpowering the wine completely. And don't forget to grab an extra bottle to pour while prepping dinner!

SEARED FISH WITH FRESH FRUIT SALSA

MIX:

2 tablespoons red wine vinegar

2 tablespoons lime juice

6 tablespoons olive oil

Dash of cumin

Honey to taste (depends on the ripeness of your fruit)

Minced shallot

Salt & Pepper

FINELY DICE, IN A PROPORTION THAT MAKES YOU HAPPY:

Banana

Plum, peach, and/or other stone fruit

Strawberries

Mango

Avocado

Red onion

Jalapeño

Cilantro

We drink 1W wines all summer long when we can pick up a piece of just-caught, flaky white fish at the market and serve it with a fresh fruit salsa. The acid in the dressing and the wine pair together perfectly. 1W wines don't always have a lot of flavor, and neither does flaky white fish. Instead, this pairing is all about lip-smacking acidity. This is our basic recipe, but the truth is we add anything that is ripe and ready to eat!

Pour enough vinaigrette over the diced fruit to flavor it, leaving extra to dress your salad greens. Meanwhile, sear the white fish filets in a hot cast iron pan, flipping once, until just cooked through. Place on a bed of greens, top with salsa, and drizzle additional vinaigrette over top. Season with salt and pepper.

PERFECT PAIRINGS

Briny oysters

Shellfish

Ceviche

White fish

Light dishes with bright acidity

FOODS TO AVOID

Cream- or butter-based dishes

ONE TO TRY

ULACIA GETARIAKO TXAKOLI (TXAKOLI, SPAIN)

A WINEMAKING REGION STEEPED in history, but not made an official D.O. (Denomination of Origin) until 1989, Getariako Txakolina produces wines that have recently caught fire in the United States. We Americans reach for them primarily in the summer months, but their lemonade acidity and slight effervescence make them a wonderful food pairing wine for lighter dishes all year long—a fact not lost on the Spanish, who consume these wines at pintxos bars, no matter the season. Getariako is the largest winemaking region in the area and exports the most wines to the U.S., but the smaller region of Bizkaiko is also worth seeking out.

You'll see the name of these Basque wines written differently from region to region, as well as country to country. Txakolina, Txakoli, and Chacoli are the most common spellings and all refer to wine made with primarily Hondarabbi Zuri grapes blended with a small amount of Hondarabbi Beltza, which is actually a red grape varietal. Txakoli, as we refer to it at The Urban Grape, is characterized by its minerality, salinity (thanks to humid ocean breezes), acidity, and spritzi-ness. Basque-influenced words are hard to pronounce. Just learn CHALK-O-LEE and you're golden.

While Txomin Etxaniz is the region's largest producer, our favorite Txakoli comes from a family-owned producer called Ulacia. There, three generations of winemakers combine their ancestral knowledge with a new winemaking facility, built in 2009. The grapes are hand harvested and then fermented in stainless steel tanks with native yeast. The carbon dioxide that occurs naturally during fermentation is purposely captured and kept in the wine, leading to the effervescence that the region is known for. By December, the wine is bottled and sent out to market—an incredibly short turnaround that ensures the wine's freshness.

You don't have to be shy with this wine: pour it hard into the glass and give it a little swirl to release the bubbles. It's low in alcohol, bone dry, and light-bodied, almost more like a lemon seltzer than wine. The initial sips dry out your mouth on the front of your palate, but almost immediately, the sides of your mouth will start watering, making you crave another sip . . . and then another. The back of the palate gets hit with something that's reminiscent of another childhood favorite: sour green apple Jolly Ranchers. All of it adds up to a wine that is just a whisper on your tongue and goes down very fast!

LET'S PAIR IT
Melon, Jamon, and Manchego Salad

Txakoli has lots of natural salinity to it, making it a good pairing with the saltiness of cheese and prosciutto. The wine's tartness also plays perfectly against something sweet, like ripe melon. **We like pairing the Ulacia with all three of these flavors in a Melon and Jamon salad.** Put down a peppery green base of arugula, which will be complemented perfectly by the green overtones of the wine, creating a playful push/pull on your palate. The acid on this one is so intense that it will make your mouth want another sip, and bite, to keep the sensation going.

MELON, JAMON, AND MANCHEGO SALAD

SERVES 4

1 ripe melon, peeled, seeded, and cut into 1-inch cubes (about 2 cups)

4 tablespoons extra virgin olive oil, divided

1 tablespoon lemon juice

½ teaspoon red pepper flakes

1 teaspoon sliced chives

Salt to taste

2 cups baby arugula

4 radishes, sliced lengthwise as thinly as possible

1½ tablespoons sherry vinegar

Freshly ground pepper to taste

¼ pound Jamon Serrano (or prosciutto), sliced as thinly as possible

3-ounce piece of Manchego, peeled into long strips

Cantaloupe, honeydew, Galia, Tuscan, watermelon—it turns out that my favorite melon is the ripest melon, so find one of those, and move on. I love French breakfast radishes, for their elegant color palette and distinctive shape, but red ones will do just fine. And any spicy green will work if you don't have arugula on hand. Really good Jamon Serrano can be hard to come by, but a good prosciutto, sliced as thin as you can get it, works just as well. When it's time to plate the dish, feather the ham and cheese onto the plate like an '80s starlet's bangs. —GABRIEL

Toss the cubed melon in a bowl with a tablespoon of the olive oil, lemon juice, red pepper flakes, and chives; season with salt to taste. Place the dressed melon cubes on a salad platter. In another bowl, lightly toss the arugula and radishes with the remaining 3 tablespoons of olive oil and sherry vinegar. Season greens with salt and pepper and place the leaves over and around the melon. Finally, feather the ham and cheese slices over the salad.

WHEN A WINE IS JUST A WINE

ON THE PROGRESSIVE SCALE, the light-bodied 2Ws are still Porch Pounders, but there is an almost imperceptible change in the heft of the wine: We've moved from ethereal to something just louder than a whisper.

We've talked about the influence of a cool growing climate on the wines in this chapter. The 2W wines are still considered cool-climate wines with alpine and maritime influence, but with one small difference. The maritime influence comes not only from the

AT A GLANCE

climate	Cool alpine- and maritime-influenced regions
regions	Finger Lakes, New York; Muscadet and Sancerre, France; Alto Adige, Italy
varietals	Riesling, Melon de Bourgogne, Sauvignon Blanc, Pinot Grigio
technique	Mostly stainless-steel fermented; but some sur lie aging
characteristics	Light-bodied with a mouthfeel resembling skim milk; bright acidity
color	Pale straw-hued
ideal pairings	Grilled shrimp and calamari; scallops ceviche; oysters; crab salad; cucumber, melon, green apple

ocean, but also from lakes, rivers, and other bodies of water. Regions like the Finger Lakes in New York, Sancerre in France, and Alto Adige in Italy have cold shoulder seasons in spring and fall, but luckily see enough temperate warmth in the summer months to support a growing season. The growing season is more challenging, with the risk of frost always on the winemaker's mind. However, a touch more warmth means more grape varietals can grow, and the 2W section begins to introduce us to some of the best-known white wine varietals in the world.

Pinot Grigio, Sauvignon Blanc, Grüner Veltliner, Riesling, Torrontes, and even Chardonnay: We'll see these wines over and over again throughout the coming chapters but they make their first appearance in 2W. How do some varietals like Chardonnay—grapes best known for producing fat and supple wines—end up as Porch Pounders? Because the ones we're going to look at are grown in less-than-perfect temperatures and in challenging soil that adds minerality but not heft. Most importantly, they're made by winemakers who stay out of the way of the wine. That's right, despite being grapes that can handle a lot of manipulation, when you see them this low on the Progressive Scale, it means the winemakers have done little more than pick, press, and bottle.

It's easy to dismiss Porch Pounders as unsophisticated wines because we often don't drink them in serious situations. The fact is, sipping them while playing cornhole in our backyard may *seem* like serious work. But who are we kidding? The reality is that because these wines have almost no winemaker manipulation, they're actually extraordinary examples of what wine can be when it's left alone to just be wine.

GEEKOUT:
WHAT ON EARTH IS TERROIR?

Terroir might be the most over-used term in wine. It has (for obvious reasons of translation) come to mean the very soil in which the grapes are grown. But the reality is that it means so much more than that.

We can't truly understand wine without talking about terroir, which is more correctly defined as the influence that soil, topography, and climate have on the grapes while they are growing; thereby imparting nuances onto the wine itself. The fact is, if you take the same grape varietal and grow it in different places, in different soils, with different climate influences, and at different terrains, you'll end up with vastly different wines. While these influences can make learning about wine more confusing, they're also the small details that keep wine lovers engaged for a lifetime.

Some wine writers will even lump a region's traditional winemaking influences (like letting grapes dry in the sun for Amarone, a practice we discuss in detail later in the book) into terroir. Mass produced wines are more formulaic (think "Coke Classic"), which is why we suggest looking for smaller producers that take their lead from the land. Terroir really is what makes wine *wine*. You'll see us reference specific terroirs, and their importance, throughout the book.

Our Favorite Regions and Varietals

Intriguing on their own, or as a pairing to food, the 2Ws at The Urban Grape span most of the influential winemaking regions of Europe, and for the first time, the Progressive Scale includes wine from the United States. Many regions, like Sancerre, first appear in this section but we will continue to feel their influence for many chapters to come. Other regions, like Txakoli, disappear completely after 2W.

FRANCE

REGION: Loire Valley
VARIETAL: Melon de Bourgogne

The diverse Loire region of France is home to Muscadet, and white wines made with the Melon de Bourgogne grape. The lightest-bodied Muscadets are crisp and clean, a shining example of 1W. The region is just as well known for producing Muscadet Sur Lie, a process that leaves the wine to age on the dead yeast cells (*lees*) that remain after fermentation. This extended contact adds body to the wine, as well as a nutty bread-yeast flavor. Remember the phrase Sur Lie, (which sounds like "sir lee"). We'll see it again before we're done with the whites, as it's a favorite technique winemakers use to add additional body to a wine.

ITALY

REGION: Alto Adige
VARIETAL: Pinot Grigio

Alto Adige, the Northern-most winemaking region in Italy, is nestled close to Austria and Switzerland, and the winegrowing there takes place up the slopes of the Italian Alps. Alto Adige brings a lot of varietals to the table, including a lesser-known favorite of ours, Kerner. But it's the region's outstanding Pinot Grigio that really appeals to the American palate. Alto Adige Pinot Grigio is like American Pinot Grigio on acid, literally. The region's wines have got so much more zip, zest, and interest than their stateside peers that they'll ruin you for all others. Not to mention, you can practically taste the alpine air. Look for wines from Alto Adige or Trentino-Alto Adige to ensure you're grabbing a 2W you'll love.

UNITED STATES

REGION: Finger Lakes, New York
VARIETAL: Riesling

And, hello America! We're not here in a big way, but at least we've sent a representative to the party. The cooler climate, lake influence, and shorter growing season of the Finger Lakes region in New York makes growing grapes a challenge. Instead of fighting their unique natural challenges, the growers of this region have smartly embraced the Riesling grape, which flourishes in these conditions. Finger Lakes Riesling is gaining credibility and accolades with every passing year. They are light-bodied Rieslings that taste great, and practically jump out of the glass with bright acidity. Not to mention, they have that underdog appeal we all love!

WHAT TO EAT WITH
— 2W WINES —

There's so much to love *about these easy-drinking wines from some of the most famous wine growing regions in the world (and some up-and-coming ones, too). Generally speaking, these wines are slightly more approachable than 1Ws, but still retain that explosive acidity.*

THE BEST GREEK SALAD EVER

LAYER THE FOLLOWING CHOPPED, SLICED, OR DICED ITEMS ON A BIG PLATTER:

A mix of lettuces, including herbs, endive, and radicchio if you have some

A mix of tomatoes, including red field, grape, and cherry

Cucumber

Avocado

Red Onion

Radishes

Roasted red peppers (homemade if you have the time)

Pitted Kalamata olives

Pepperoncini

Feta cheese

Herbed croutons (again, homemade if you can)

Lemon-soaked chicken, grilled

Greek Vinaigrette

By far the most requested Douglas family recipe from May to October, this dish even hits our table in the dead of winter when we're sick of stew. It's great as a family meal because our kids eat a deconstructed version with just the foods they like. The coastally influenced wines of 2W have a salinity that pairs perfectly with the briny feta cheese and olives.

For the chicken: The morning of, cut your chicken breasts in half lengthwise and coat with 2 cloves minced garlic, 1 teaspoon salt, 1 teaspoon pepper, lots of chopped oregano, and the juice of 2 to 3 lemons. Refrigerate until dinnertime. Grill just before serving.

For the dressing: Combine 3 tablespoons red wine vinegar, juice from a whole lemon, olive oil equal to the vinegar and lemon, a clove or two of garlic, minced, and 1 tablespoon chopped oregano. This is a really acidic dressing, which we love. If it's too much acid for you, just add more olive oil.

PERFECT PAIRINGS

Grilled shrimp or calamari

Lightly dressed crab salad

Oysters

Scallops—in ceviche or grilled

Cucumbers, melon, green apple

FOODS TO AVOID

Cream- or butter-based dishes

ONE TO TRY

CLAUDE RIFFAULT "LES CHASSEIGNES" SANCERRE (LOIRE VALLEY, FRANCE)

OH, SANCERRE. You're a perfect example of how terroir influences a widely known and almost ubiquitous grape, Sauvignon Blanc, and turns it into something utterly sublime. At The Urban Grape you'll find Sancerre on the wall anywhere from 2W to 4W, with the only real difference being the soil in which it's grown. Winemakers can and do influence the body of the wine in production, but the differences originate in the soil.

Sancerre, a growing region in the Loire Valley of France, has a fossil-rich vein of Kimmeridgean Clay running underneath it that dates back to the Jurassic age. The region is best known for having three different soil types: Silex (flint), Les Caillottes (gravel and limestone), and Terre Blanche (clay and chalk). Each imparts distinct nuances on the wine that affect its fragrance, taste, and body. Typically, the lightest-bodied Sancerre wines are grown in Silex and Les Caillotes soils, and the heaviest-bodied in Terre Blanche. But remember: It's all relative. These wines are all light-bodied compared to the wines we'll see in later chapters.

Domaine Claude Riffault is now owned and managed by Claude's son, Stéphane Riffault, the fifth generation to work the family's many parcels. Despite his relatively young age compared to other producers in the area, Stéphane has quickly made his mark, producing wines that capture the true essence of Sancerre and its varied terroir, all while instituting organic farming and bringing a modern sensibility to his wines. He's not afraid to look to neighboring Burgundy, where his brother Benoit is also a winemaker, for some tips on employing hand-harvesting and sorting, as well as using some light, neutral oak, to bring out the best in his wines. Thanks to these influences, some of his wines have more

aging potential than other producers from this region.

All of Stéphane's Sancerres are fantastic, and we highly recommend seeking them out and tasting them side by side for a master class on terroir and how it affects the body and flavor of a wine. His "Les Chasseignes," grown in the shallow and gravelly Les Caillottes limestone soil, is an especially good example of a 2W wine at The Urban Grape. Important for any Porch Pounder, it's meant to be enjoyed young, and stands on its own as an aperitif. (Although, Stéphane argues, it's also a perfect pairing for the region's Crottin de Chavignol goat cheese.) The aromas of the wine are striking and pretty: floral, fruity, fragrant. A light touch of barrel aging on half of the wine tames the harshest edges of the acid, but you won't taste any wood on the palate. It's fresh and bright from the front to the finish.

LET'S PAIR IT
Oysters with Campari Italian Ice

Sancerre is famous for having aromas that make you weak in the knees. With stony minerality, citrusy fruit aromas, and herbaceous overtones, these wines are expressive and lively. **Briny oysters bring out the best in the Riffault Sancerre, especially when topped with an easy-to-make Campari ice.** The lemon and grapefruit juices in the Campari ice are mirrored in the wine. The bitterness of the Campari works beautifully with the minerality of Sancerre, giving structure to the pairing. Both the wine and oysters have a briny salinty, creating a perfect, joyful pairing.

OYSTERS
with CAMPARI ITALIAN ICE

SERVES 4

1 cup fresh pink
grapefruit juice

¾ cup fresh lemon juice

½ cup Campari

¾ cup simple syrup

1 shallot, finely diced

Pinch of salt

1 teaspoon cracked
black pepper

2 dozen fresh East
Coast oysters

Olive oil

1 tablespoon thinly
sliced chives

When choosing oysters for this dish, the brinier the better—the salt will hold up well against the Campari. I also implore you to do the juicing of the citrus yourself. And simple syrup is just that—an easy 1-to-1 combination of water to sugar. Heat the mixture until the sugar is dissolved, and let cool before using.   —GABRIEL

In a large bowl, mix the grapefruit and lemon juices, Campari, simple syrup, shallot, salt, and pepper together. Pour into a shallow, flat metal pan and freeze overnight. When ready to serve, use the front of a fork to scrape the ice into layers so that it resembles shaved ice, taking care to scrape all the way down to the bottom (the mixture will separate during the freezing process). Put the shaved ice into a pint container and return to the freezer while shucking the oysters. Once the oysters are shucked, spoon the Campari ice over each oyster and add a dash of olive oil and a pinch of chives. Reserve any excess ice in the freezer for a later use.

HOW TO LEARN MORE ABOUT WINE

Learning about wine can be intimidating. We understand that. It's a vast world, and lots of what is in it is an acquired taste. The names of the varietals are confusing; the regions require a master's degree in geography; and the endeavor to explore can be time-consuming and expensive. It's no wonder that the vast majority of wine drinkers buy the same bottle time and time again, never varying from their tried and true. So, how can you learn to *Drink Progressively?*

Vow to Explore

As tempting as it is to buy cases of your favorite wine, and drink only that for the next year, promise instead to reach for a new bottle as often as you can. It doesn't need to be a more expensive bottle, it just needs to be something different. Maybe it's a new producer from an importer that you trust; or a new varietal from a winemaker whose wines you like. Keep notes on what you appreciate about the wine, and also what doesn't taste good to you. But try, try, try.

Start Reading

Reading about wine seems like a non-starter. After all, wine is all about taste! But reading will help you start to organize the maze of varietals and regions, and provide a jumping off place for when you are tasting. Wine books, like this one and classics like Kevin Zraly's *Windows on the World*, are invaluable; but, there are also great blogs like *Wine Folly* and newspaper columns like Erik Asimov's *The Pour* that provide clear paths to learning. Magazines like *Food & Wine, Bon Appetit,* and *Wine Spectator* also cover popular trends and make it easy to try new bottles with confidence.

Make Date Night a Tasting Night

Most communities have adult education centers, which are excellent resources for wine classes. Bigger cities, like Boston, even have wine schools at varied levels of commitment from single classes to semester-long

studies. If you can't find a class where you live, start your own! Gather some friends, choose a varietal, read up on the subject, and have everyone bring a different bottle to try. Taste through them with and without food, and then blind taste them, too. It doesn't have to be formal to be an education!

Find a Local Store You Trust

Most independently owned wine shops want to help you learn more about wine. At UG, we offer three free tastings a week, as well as more in-depth classes. This is your chance to try new wines and learn about them—all for free and with no commitment! While big box stores do free tastings as well, you'll find better quality and more knowledge at the smaller shops.

Travel

You don't need to fly to Italy to learn about wine. Almost every state in the U.S. is producing wine these days. Sure, some states make better wine than others, but that doesn't mean you can't visit a local winery and learn more about the winemaking process. If you can get out of the country, plan ahead to reserve a tour and tasting at local wineries near your destination. Tasting a wine where it was made always helps you understand that elusive meaning of terroir, and seeing the grapes on the vine, the winemaking facilities, and the work that goes into production is inspiring.

CHAPTER 2

FRUIT JOINS THE PARTY

Just like you might start to tire of a summer romance that's hung around too long, you can't live your life drinking only Porch Pounders. Eventually, you're going to want a wine with more substance, drive, passion, and focus (i.e. lifelong mate material). The wines in sections 3W and 4W bring you just that—all while remaining utterly drinkable and fresh, with lively acidity throughout. 3W wines remain fairly light-bodied, but by the time we get to Chapter Three and the 5W section, we'll be delving in to "whole milk" territory. So, hang on tight because things on the Progressive Scale are about to change quickly.

TASTE THE SUNSHINE

IN OUR HOME, we are equal opportunity drinkers. We truly believe there is a time, a place, and a meal for wine from every section of The Urban Grape's Progressive Scale. To pick a favorite section would be like picking a favorite song—just as soon as you fall in love with one tune, you turn on the radio and another one takes its place.

While we love to bounce around (and encourage our customers, and now you through this book, to do the same), the American white wine palate seems stubbornly auto-tuned to 3W wines. And frankly, we understand the passion. 3W is where the grapes seem to come alive, and where you can start to taste the sunshine.

AT A GLANCE

climate	Slightly warmer and sunnier regions; primarily alpine- and maritime-influenced
regions	Tuscany and Campania, Italy; Alsace, France; Willamette Valley, Oregon; Marlborough, New Zealand; Napa Valley, California
varietals	Vernaccia, Falanghina, Riesling, Pinot Grigio/Gris, Sauvignon Blanc
technique	Primarily steel fermented; some aging in concrete eggs or neutral-oak barrels; some sur lie
characteristics	Between light and medium body with increased fruit and texture and a mouthfeel of 1% milk; vibrant acidity
color	Pale yellow
ideal pairings	Sushi; spring vegetables; aromatic herbs; white meat and firm white fish; soft, mild cheeses

Geographically, we've moved out of the coolest growing regions in the world and into more temperate zones. The regions are seeing moderate sunshine and warmth, and as a result, grapes with slightly thicker skins start to burst onto the scene. These hardier grapes take longer to ripen, and when they are pressed after harvest, their skins give the wine more texture and interest. Already, we're starting to build body—but that's not all that's coming into play.

We've also got more sugar. It's helpful to start thinking of the grapes as little body builders. When the sun shines down on the grapes, their little grape muscles are pumping up the sugar production. These sugars ultimately influence the body of the wine. At night, when the sun goes down and the temperatures cool, the grapes rest and rebuild. The rebuilding time is what allows the grape to develop and maintain acid alongside the sugar. 3W wines still have a lot of bright acid on the palate, but thanks to the sun, now we've got fruit, too. It's this perfect balance of zippy freshness and fruit aromas that so intrigues the American palate.

Here's what we're still *not* seeing: wines from really hot climates and too much winemaker manipulation. Some of these 3W wines might have extended lees contact or neutral oak aging in big *foudres* (giant oak tanks that allow for oxygenation, which builds texture, but doesn't impart much wood tannin or flavor), but for the most part, 3W wines are aged in stainless steel and bottled young and fresh. Winemakers are primarily just stewards of the process.

These wines have a lot going on—complex acidity, bright aromas, and fresh fruit nuances on the palate. It's no wonder they're considered some of the best food pairing wines available, and a favorite of wine drinkers around the world.

GEEKOUT: TAMING THE SWEET TOOTH, A.K.A. RESIDUAL SUGAR

First, let's review. During fermentation, yeast eats the sugar in the grape's juice to produce alcohol, carbon dioxide, and sulfites. In Chapter One, we looked at cooler climate grapes that contained less sugar; therefore, they have lower alcohol levels after fermentation. However, as we move into 3W, we have to start learning about residual sugar and its effects on a finished wine.

Knowing what we do, it makes sense that warmer weather and more sun produce grapes with more sugar. The winemakers have a choice: Let the yeast eat all of the sugar, which produces a dry, yet higher alcohol, wine; or, stop fermentation and produce a wine with some residual sugar, which is thereby sweeter. This winemaker wiggle room is why we see grape varietals in this and other sections that can be produced in dry, semi-sweet, or sweet styles. Wines with more residual sugar often feel like they have more body and texture because the additional glycerine gives a chewiness to the wine.

The key to making residual sugar palatable is for winemakers to maintain healthy levels of acidity in the wine. Without acidity, and other offsetting factors like tannin and minerality, wines with residual sugar can taste viscous and flabby.

Our Favorite Regions and Varietals

Part of the reason why the American palate is so enamored by 3W is because of our nationwide love of Sauvignon Blanc. Indeed, Sauvignon Blanc wines from France, New Zealand, and California are the staples of the 3W section and intrigue wine palates across the world. Bright, zesty, and aromatic— no one will argue if you reach for a Sauvignon Blanc.

UNITED STATES

REGION: Napa Valley, California
VARIETAL: Sauvignon Blanc

If you want to explore Sauvignon Blanc outside of the world-famous region of Sancerre, we suggest two New World options: California and New Zealand. There is excellent Sauvignon Blanc throughout Napa Valley, and some of our favorites come from the Rutherford AVA, where the weather is influenced by winds off the ocean and early morning fog. Clean, crisp, and refreshing, these Sauvignon Blanc wines have lots of acidity that is balanced by lush fruit. If you can't find Rutherford, wines from the other AVAs of Napa are a good choice, particularly those grown in St. Helena. However, make sure to look for a quality producer that has taken the time to let the minerality and acidity of the wine shine through.

NEW ZEALAND

REGION: Marlborough
VARIETAL: Sauvignon Blanc

The Marlborough region in New Zealand has become synonymous with Sauvignon Blanc thanks to the raging popularity of brands like Cloudy Bay and Kim Crawford. But to miss out on the smaller producers of this region would be a travesty, because over the years these winemakers have become experts at harnessing the region's unique minerality. Bright days with almost endless sunshine, combined with cool nights, produce grapes with both vibrant fruit and acid. Known for a stunning combination of "grass and grapefruit" there is nothing quite like a Sauvignon Blanc from this region. Taking the time to get beyond the mainstream will reward your senses greatly!

ITALY

REGION: Campania
VARIETAL: Falanghina

Italy may be best known for its red wines, but the country does light-bodied white wines incredibly well, and produces many of our favorite non-Sauvignon Blanc varietals. Vermentino lives in 3W and 4W, but we'll focus on it more in the next section. For us, 3W is all about Falanghina from Campania, located in the "shoe-laces" of Italy's boot, just above Sicily. Our favorite appellation, known as a DOC in Italy, is Falanghina del Sannio, which produces wines with floral aromatics, a fruity palate, and vibrant acidity and minerality. Falanghina is an approachable, palate-friendly wine, and is almost always affordably priced.

WHAT TO EAT WITH
— 3W WINES —

Warmer climates and sunnier days *lead to wines with enhanced fruit flavors, herbal nuances, and increased texture on the palate. Generally speaking, these wines are very drinkable and enjoyable, and pair incredibly well with a wide variety of foods, as long as the dishes themselves are not too heavy or overpowering.*

SUSHI NIGHT!

If our kids are at a sleepover, then their least favorite food, sushi, is on our table. Sushi and sake are a natural pairing and always taste great together, but there continues to be intimidation around how to choose and serve sake. Therefore, we also suggest serving sushi with 3W wines, whose mouthfeel and body are the most similar to that of sake.

The 3W wines have enough flavor and acidity to stand up to the fat from the fish and the saltiness of the soy sauce without overpowering the other, more delicate flavors. Thanks to their natural fruitiness, 3W wines pair particularly well with rolls that have additional elements, like cucumber, avocado, and mango.

PERFECT PAIRINGS

Soft cheeses

....

Spring vegetables

....

Aromatic herbs and delicate spices

....

White meat protein

....

Firmer white fish and shellfish

FOODS TO AVOID

Red sauce pasta dishes

ONE TO TRY

ALEXANA RIESLING (WILLAMETTE VALLEY, OREGON)

SIX HUNDRED MILES NORTH OF NAPA, in Oregon's Dundee Hills AVA, the Alexana Winery—sister to the Revana Winery in Napa and Corazon del Sol winery in Mendoza, Argentina—is snuggled inside a series of protective ridges and fertile valleys. It's here that Dr. Madaiah Revana, a renowned cardiologist in Houston, has combined the farming legacy of his family in India with his love of wine. He has vineyards in Napa that focus primarily on Cabernet Sauvignon and grew out of his love for the First Growths of Bordeaux. In Oregon, his team, including winemaker Bryan Weil and consulting winemaker Lynn Penner-Ash, focuses mostly on Pinot Noir, in homage to the wines of Burgundy.

Most of this sustainably farmed Oregon property is warm and temperate, shielded from the region's cooling fog by a series of ridges that line the property. Warm days combined with incredible soil variation throughout the vineyards make this perfect Pinot Noir growing territory. Lucky for us, a cooler microclimate found here is also a welcome home for the finicky and hard-to-grow Riesling grape. The resulting Revana wine has become one of our favorite American-made Rieslings.

Let's pause and talk about Riesling, the darling of the sommelier set and yet a wine that causes confusion among us common folk. Sometimes sweet, sometimes off-dry, sometimes bone dry, sometimes light-bodied, sometimes heavy-bodied—choosing a bottle of Riesling can feel like playing a game of Russian Roulette. Faced with spending our hard earned cash on a bottle of wine, most of us move on to a varietal that doesn't wear as many faces.

But it's precisely this versatility that, once understood, makes Riesling such a perfect food-pairing wine. The easiest cheat is to look at the ABV, or alcohol by volume, on the bottle. Rieslings with higher ABV (11-13%) are typically bracingly dry with high acid and a lighter body. Cold and briny shellfish are a natural pairing. Off-dry Rieslings come in around 10% ABV, and, despite having some sweetness, they are never cloying because they still exhibit the grape's backbone of acid. If spicy food is on your plate, an off-dry Riesling should be in your glass. Pairing cheese or dessert? Grab a low-alcohol (8% ABV) Riesling. The grapes for these wines have been left on the vine to ripen longer, meaning they have higher levels of residual sugar, and therefore sweetness.

One of the most famous dry Riesling regions is Alsace, France. (Many will argue that Rheingau, Germany is *the* most world-renowned region.) Known for their aromatics, lively acidity, and petrol quality (yes, really, petrol . . . this sounds off-putting, we realize, but we promise it's pleasant!), these are some of the best food-pairing wines in the world. Lucky for us, the Alexana Riesling is Alsatian in style, and an easy-to-find wine. This is one bottle you can grab with confidence!

LET'S PAIR IT

Basil Salad with Almond Vinaigrette and Candied Lemon

The slightly off-dry Alexana Riesling (the alcohol level is 11.2%), has elements of sweetness to it, but you'd never confuse it with a dessert wine. **The hint of sweetness and expressive acid in this Riesling pair beautifully with salads that feature the same flavor profile, our favorite of which is Gabriel's Basil Salad with Candied Lemons.** You'll notice that the delicate citrusy sweetness of the wine is mirrored perfectly in the sweet citrus flavors of the lemons. Both the wine and salad are deceptively delicate, and either could be overpowered by the wrong pairing. Instead, this beautiful combination brings out the best in both the dish and the wine.

BASIL SALAD

SERVES 4

with **ALMOND VINAIGRETTE AND CANDIED LEMON**

BASIL SALAD WITH ALMOND VINAIGRETTE

6 ounces baby spinach, cleaned and dried

3 ounces mixed basil, cleaned and dried

2 tablespoons honey

⅓ cup Sherry or Champagne vinegar

1 cup almond or grapeseed oil

Kosher salt and freshly cracked black pepper

2 ounces salted almonds, chopped

¼ cup Candied Lemon (recipe below)

CANDIED LEMON

2 regular lemons (or 3 to 4 Meyer lemons)

½ cup sugar

¼ teaspoon finishing salt, such as Maldon's or other large crystal salt

I like using a mix of different types of basil for this salad, ideally a combination of Genovese (your regular sweet basil), opal, and Thai—but using only standard basil won't disappoint. Similarly, I'll advocate for Marcona almonds, and gladly tolerate any salted almond. You'll likely have extra dressing and candied lemon leftover—both will keep in the refrigerator, stored in separate airtight containers. (The lemons also make a great garnish for cocktails!) —GABRIEL

In a large mixing bowl, combine the spinach and basil. In a medium-sized mixing bowl, combine the honey and vinegar. Whisk to combine, and continue whisking while slowly adding the almond or grapeseed oil in a thin stream, to form an emulsified vinaigrette.

Drizzle a small a tablespoon of the vinaigrette along the inside of the large mixing bowl, just above the greens. Gently toss the greens in the bowl, and then season lightly with salt and pepper. Add half of the almonds, half of the Candied Lemon, and a little more vinaigrette. Again, gently toss and then taste for seasoning and dressing. The basil and spinach should look shiny but not laden with oil; a light hand works best. Transfer the salad to individual plates and garnish with remaining lemon and almonds. Serve immediately.

CANDIED LEMON

Using a sharp vegetable peeler, peel the lemons from top to bottom in long strips; reserve the peels. Juice lemons and reserve 2 tablespoons of the lemon juice. Using a paring knife, remove as much of the pith (white) from the rind (yellow) as possible, by laying the peels skin side down and cutting off the pith. Place all of the cleaned peels in a medium pot and cover with cold water. Blanch the peels by bringing the water just to a boil, then quickly drain. Repeat the process two more times. Cover with cold water once more, add the sugar, and bring to a boil. Reduce the heat slightly and boil slowly until the mixture is very sticky. Remove from the heat and add the salt and reserved lemon juice. Using a slotted spoon, place the peels on a cooling rack or piece of parchment paper. Pour the remaining syrup into a small container with a lid. Once the peels are cool enough to handle, use a sharp knife to julienne the peels. Once all of the peel is julienned, store it in the container with the syrup and refrigerate until ready to use.

FRIDAY NIGHT WHITES

WE'RE REACHING THE END OF THE LINE for grapes just being grapes. As we move up on the Progressive Scale, we'll start to see how winemakers impart more and more influence over the wine in our glass. That transition starts with 4W wines. Here, we see grapes from all over the world, but our favorites are from the Mediterranean region. The biggest change from earlier in the book is that we start to see neutral fermentation and aging techniques. We also delve into the wine world's hottest topic at the moment: natural wine.

Foudres, those giant oak barrels we told you about in 3W, are considered a neutral

AT A GLANCE

climate	A mix of warm and cool climates; some Mediterranean ocean influences
regions	Alsace, Burgundy, and Loire Valley, France; Tuscany, Italy; Columbia Valley, Washington; Stajerska, Slovenia; Willamette Valley, Oregon; Niederösterreich, Austria
varietals	Riesling, Chardonnay, Chenin Blanc, Vermentino, Semillon, Pinot Grigio/Gris, Grüner Veltliner
technique	Some winemaker influence using sur lie aging, light skin contact, and/or neutral wood aging; no malolactic fermentation (ML)
characteristics	Enhanced body, texture, and complexity with sweeter fruit nuances and a mouthfeel of 2% milk
color	Yellow with golden hues
ideal pairings	Light pasta dishes; Mediterranean dishes; firm, fatty fish; grilled chicken sausages; spicy take-out food

aging agent, but they're still important tools for winemakers. A staple for many lighter bodied red wines, *foudres* are now becoming popular with white wines, too. *Foudres* can be used continuously for decades, but after five years they're considered oak neutral; therefore, their purpose is not to impart flavor into the wine. The wood slats, or staves as they are called, are thin enough to allow for some very gentle body-building oxygenation of the wine, but thick enough to keep the wines from becoming overly oxidized. (Too much oxygen is a wine-killer—just leave a bottle open on your counter for a few days and see!) *Foudres* are the perfect solution for light-bodied white wines that would be overwhelmed by too much oak, but benefit from a little time in vat before bottling.

Another rising trend for wines in this section is the use of concrete eggs for fermentation and aging, instead of stainless steel tanks. White wine producers are really hot on using concrete eggs right now—it's an ancient winemaking technique that is roaring back onto the scene throughout wine regions across the world. Cement eggs (they look pretty much exactly how they sound: large, smooth, concrete vessels) are just porous enough to allow for gentle oxygenation and a boost to the body and mouthfeel of the wine. The thick concrete also keeps white wines cool and protects the juice from fermentation-busting temperature spikes. This allows winemakers to more easily control levels of sugar and alcohol. Concrete also preserves acidity—a vital component in this section, now that we are seeing more rich, tropical fruit flavors in these wines—and many winemakers believe that concrete enhances the minerality of a wine. And, there's one more benefit that's purely for Mother Earth: With oak tree shortages across the world and cooperages scrambling to find trees with which to make their barrels, concrete eggs are saving the day.

4Ws are the perfect TGIF wine. Light enough to enjoy by themselves, but effortlessly paired with all sorts of food, they make a welcome, and easy, end to the work week!

GEEKOUT: DECODING THE NATURAL WINE TREND

Get any group of people in the wine industry together, and the topic quickly turns to the natural wine trend. Some scoff, some ponder, some embrace. If anything, the loosely defined parameters cause confusion and frustration. Here's how we define natural wine at The Urban Grape: an organically or biodynamically produced wine with minimal winemaker intervention. Natural wine makers boast that their wines display more terroir, and in general we agree. Some of these wines are life changing, but some make you gag. That said, we feel the same way about most wine on the market! The truth is, there is room for all thoughtfully made wine, no matter the designation.

In general, natural wine techniques, like aging on the skins and open-top fermentation (for white wine), whole-cluster fermentation, and not adding sulfites (for white and red wines), do produce wines with interesting mouthfeel and body. So, what matters to us is where to find them on the Progressive Scale. At UG, natural white wines cluster around 4W. You rarely see them higher, because techniques like oak aging are frowned upon. As always, what matters most is whether or not YOU like the wine! By exploring natural wines, you'll soon learn what techniques you do and don't like, and will be able to define your own parameters for the natural wine trend.

Our Favorite Regions and Varietals

Close your eyes and stick a pin on a map. If you're in Europe, you're probably pretty close to a 4W winemaking region: Tuscany, Sardinia, Sicily, Northern Italy, Greece, Slovenia, and Croatia are all home to varietals of white wine that have some roundness to them without winemaker manipulation. Mediterranean-influenced regions really shine here. The sunny warmth, briny breezes, and interesting soil compositions add up to grapes that make great, naturally medium-bodied wine.

FRANCE

REGION: Alsace
VARIETAL: Riesling

Alsace, a small border region between France and Germany, has a long history of being traded between the two countries, and as such, seems to consider itself independent of both. The Germanic influence is seen in their dedication to producing Riesling, a historically German grape. The best Alsatian Rieslings are vinified to be dry, not sweet, and have never-ending aromas that jump out of the glass. Despite being a grape that loves to produce sugar, our favorite examples lack all sweetness, and are instead punctuated by acidity and minerality.

AUSTRIA

REGION: Niederösterreich
VARIETAL: Grüner Veltliner

Longitudinally equal with Alsace, but 900 miles away, is the Austrian winemaking region of Niederösterreich (Lower Austria). Despite being separated by Germany, Alsace and Niederösterreich share a general affinity for dry vinification over sweet. Austria has a passion for Grüner Veltliner, and we like to help our customers embrace this versatile, easy-drinking, if not easily pronounced, varietal. Grüner is not known for its aromatics as much as it is for its intense acidity and herbal spiciness. It's a perfect take-out food pairing!

UNITED STATES

REGION: Willamette Valley, Oregon
VARIETAL: Pinot Gris

Some amazing winemaking is happening north of California in the Willamette Valley of Oregon. The climate and soil deposits from the Missoula Floods have made this a haven for Pinot Noir production—so much so, that sometimes the region's white wines are overlooked, especially Pinot Gris. Over half of the region's estates use sustainable farming and cement eggs to allow the true nature of both grape and terroir to come through. Expect a palate of citrus and stone fruit, minerality, and lush acidity.

WHAT TO EAT WITH
— 4W WINES —

The 4W wines are a bit of a mixed bag from both warm and cool climates, *and because of this, they pair with a wide variety of foods. However, there is rarely any malolactic fermentation yet, so these wines still don't take to creamy dishes or heavier "winter foods." 4W wines love take-out, so if you don't feel like cooking, grab something with a little spice and dig in.*

HARVEST BOWL SALAD

Long grain rice (I make 1½ cups for four people so I can have leftovers)

Lacinato kale, stripped off the stem and cut into thin ribbons

Several sweet, firm apples, chopped

Sweet potato, cubed and roasted (just in the fall and winter months)

Pecans (toasted or not, your preference)

Dried cranberries

Feta or goat cheese

Lemon-soaked chicken (recipe on page 37)

We have a Sweetgreen salad addiction, but running out to grab a salad for dinner isn't always convenient. So, I figured out a way to knock off our favorite salad, the Harvest Bowl. It's our youngest son Jason's favorite meal, and every time I make it TJ declares: "I could eat this every single night." It pairs with a wide variety of whites and reds, but the versatile 4W wines let the flavors of the salad shine, making the wine happy to play a supporting role in the pairing. Don't tell Sweetgreen, but we think our salad is just a little bit better.

Layer all ingredients in the desired proportions in a bowl. (Everyone in our family likes it a little differently.) Top with a honey mustard dressing, store bought or easily made. I combine 4 tablespoons apple cider vinegar, 8 to 10 tablespoons of olive oil, lots of chopped garlic, 2 big spoonfuls of honey mustard, and salt and pepper to taste.

PERFECT PAIRINGS

Firmer, fattier fish

Lighter pasta dishes

Grilled chicken sausages

Mediterranean dishes

Spicy food – especially take-out!

FOODS TO AVOID

Foods with lots of umami

ONE TO TRY

LA SPINETTA VERMENTINO (TUSCANY, ITALY)

THE HEART AND SOUL OF LA SPINETTA is owner and winemaker Giorgio Rivetti. Dedicated to winemaking since he was 16, Giorgio returned from wine apprenticeships in France to helm his family's vineyards. Under his direction, they expanded from producing only Moscato to growing Italy's indigenous grapes in vineyards throughout Piedmont and Tuscany.

La Spinetta is best known for its red wines: Barolo, Barbaresco, Langhe Nebbiolo, and Barbera. To profile this winery without mentioning the reds (and insisting that you track them down and try them) would be a travesty. But if we had to pick one bottle of wine to drink for the rest of our lives on the oft-mentioned desert island, it would be La Spinetta's Vermentino.

Vermentino is a Mediterranean grape in both location and spirit. Grown most typically in Sardinia, it does well wherever it can pick up a little ocean influence to bring out its natural acidity. While it is typically a lighter bodied wine, it can be finished with some malolactic fermentation (we'll get to that, don't worry!) to add heft. That said, most of the body occurs naturally from oiliness in the grape, which is captured on the mouthfeel. The La Spinetta Vermentino is approachable, yet complex; nuanced, yet relatable. Each vintage is slightly different, but year after year, it's a perfect bottle of wine.

La Spinetta Vermentino is also an example of a wine that is generally unrecognized by the natural wine movement. Giorgio grows only historic Italian varietals. He farms organically, despite not having an official designation, and uses only naturally occurring yeasts to start fermentation in his Vermentino. He believes that ninety percent of winemaking is done in the field, and that his job is simply to shepherd the process from harvest to bottling, with minimal intervention. Sounds pretty natural, right? Well, because of the size, scale, and modern facilities of La Spinetta, few, if any, would tag this Vermentino as "natural wine." It's not quite hip and funky enough. And yet, thousands of Old World producers in Europe were making, and still do make, wine in this fashion, long before it was coined as a movement. We'll let you decide if it is a natural wine!

LET'S PAIR IT
Pear and Celery Salad

Vermentino is a wonderful food wine because the experience is ultimately more about its naturally round and meaty texture than it is about any specific flavor of the wine. But because that's the grape's natural texture, without seeing lees contact or oak aging, the wine is still fresh on the palate. **Crunchy, salty, and fatty salads like the following Pear and Celery coimbination make the La Spinetta Vermentino come alive.** The salty pecorino brings out the Mediterranean Ocean's influence on the wine, while the fat from the walnuts and cheese pair with the wine's fleshy roundness. This salad is all about dichotomies—crunchy and soft, sweet and salty—and the wine doesn't get in the way of this, instead enhancing every bite.

PEAR AND CELERY SALAD

SERVES 4

6 stalks celery, washed

1 small fennel bulb, outer layer and stalk removed

Kosher salt and freshly ground black pepper

2 tablespoons extra virgin olive oil, plus more for finishing

1 tablespoon lemon juice

2 ripe pears

¼ cup toasted walnuts, coarsely chopped

1 tablespoon pecorino, grated, plus 2 tablespoons pecorino, shaved

Ideally, I like this salad with a mix of Bartlett and Asian pears, but anything that is currently ripe will work. For the cheese, go with a younger pecorino (Romano cheese is a little too fatty for this variation). —GABRIEL

Remove leaves from celery stalks and set aside. On a cutting board, lay the celery stalks hollow side down, and slice them on the bias a little less than a ¼-inch thick. Place the slices in a large mixing bowl. Remove the fennel fronds. Cut the fennel bulb in half lengthwise, and using the tip of your knife, remove the bulk of the core by making a wedge-shaped cut. Using a mandolin or a very sharp chef's knife, slice the fennel lengthwise about half as thin as you cut the celery. Add the fennel slices to the mixing bowl. Season the celery and fennel mixture aggressively with salt and pepper. Add half of the olive oil and lemon juice and toss to combine. Taste for seasoning, noting that this salad takes a healthy amount of salt, and adjust if necessary. Cut the pears into quarters; cut away and discard the core and seeds. Using a mandolin or very sharp chef's knife, slice the pear to the same thickness as the fennel. Add the pear and walnuts to the salad, plus a little of the remaining olive oil and lemon juice. Toss the salad gently. Taste again and adjust seasoning as needed. Add the grated pecorino, the reserved celery leaves, and toss the salad again. Add remaining olive oil, lemon juice, and/or salt if needed. Serve the salad immediately topped with shaved pecorino.

ENTERTAINING AT HOME

TJ and I love to entertain at home. From impromptu dinner parties, to summer barbecues, to our annual holiday Champagne and Capture the Flag party, we are happiest when our home is filled with people. TJ is the consummate host, effortlessly filling glasses and holding court. I love bouncing between the kitchen and intimate conversations with friends. There's always home-cooked food and a tasty array of beverages. The goal is to make it look effortless. Here are our tricks to pulling it off.

Keep the Beverages Simple

Too many choices make more work for you and confusion for your guests. For most parties, we do a white (or rosé) and red wine, and beer. For more festive occasions we add a pre-batched signature cocktail, usually in punch form, that our guests can serve themselves.

Plan Ahead So You Don't Run Out

For most parties, a good rule of thumb is to plan on two drinks per person per hour. With four glasses of wine per bottle, it's easy to do the math from there. Plan on more if it's a holiday party or a destination event; plan on less for a brunch or daytime baby shower. And unless your goal is for your guests to get absolutely snookered, limit access to hard alcohol and shots. (Hey, sometimes it's fun to break into the whiskey cabinet, but no one wants to deal with "that" guest . . . or *be* that guest!)

Don't Forget the Ice

You always need more ice than you think you will. Get crushed ice to keep bottles cold, and cubed ice for drinks. If you hope to return unopened wine bottles to the store, get clear plastic sleeves to protect the labels from the ice.

Rent Everything

Nothing is worse than waking up to a hundred dirty glasses. When you rent, you can load the glasses back into the crates and leave them outside for pick-up. Easy. Don't go crazy with your rentals, either. Rocks glasses work for water, punch, and even beer from kegs or growlers. A basic wine glass works for white and red. And never fear the red Solo cup, which works for everything in a pinch. Keep it simple.

Choose Delivery

Have your local wine store deliver your wine and beer to you chilled. It makes life so much easier. Some will even deliver ice, as well.

Establish a Budget

Once you know your party budget, don't blow it all on the wine, but don't cheap out either. Pick moderately priced, palate-friendly wines from lesser-known regions to stretch your dollar. In general, pick wines that are not "too" anything: too oaky, too big, too tannic, too obscure. Look for food-friendly, medium-bodied wines that are fruit-forward and approachable. If your mom is coming, and she absolutely must have Chardonnay, get her some. But otherwise, ask your local store to help you find one white and one red to please them all (or at least most of them).

Set the Scene

Set up a gorgeous bar with lots of glassware, some fresh flowers, and candles, and commit to checking it a few times throughout the evening to restock and neaten the area; but don't feel the need to bartend or micromanage. Instead, after helping them with their first selection, let your guests gather there to meet, mingle, and serve themselves. Your job is to grab bottles and refill the glasses of guests who are immersed in conversations—it's a great way to circulate and see everyone.

Don't Cry Over Spilled Wine

Ever. Accidents happen, and everything can be fixed in the morning. We promise!

CHAPTER 3

WINEMAKERS TAKE THE REINS

Up until this point on the Progressive Scale, the wine in your glass has largely arrived to you in its natural state. The biggest influencers have been the growing climate, the grape varietal, and the different sugar and acid ratios. There are exceptions of course, like lees contact, and neutral-barrel fermentation, but for the most part, what you see is what you get. The winemakers are primarily focused on farming, harvesting, and crushing the grapes, and then fermenting and bottling the juice. Chapter Three is where the story begins to change, and winemakers start reaching into their bag of tricks for age-old winemaking techniques that add body and structure to the wine.

NATURE VERSUS NURTURE

WE'RE HALF WAY UP THE PROGRESSIVE Scale! That means we've moved from wines that have a body like skim milk to wines with a body more like whole milk. If that sentence confuses you, take a minute to do a milk taste test. Starting with skim milk, analyze the body of the milk as it hits the front of your tongue. Now, try it with whole milk, and don't be afraid to take a big gulp and swish it around in your mouth. Then, go back and forth between the two. It's a huge difference, right? As your tasting palate develops, you'll be able to distinguish this same variation in wine, and you'll develop natural preferences that have little to do with region or varietal,

AT A GLANCE

climate	A mix of cool and warm regions
regions	Napa Valley and Santa Barbara County, California; Bordeaux, Languedoc-Roussillon, and Burgundy, France; Mosel Valley, Germany; Le Marche, Italy
varietals	Sauvignon Blanc, Semillon, Grenache Blanc, Marsanne, Chardonnay, Riesling, Verdicchio
technique	A light-handed mix of techniques including residual sugar, partial malolactic fermentation, and minimal oak aging
characteristics	Softer texture and smooth finish; enhanced fruit, refreshing acidity, and a mouthfeel of whole milk
color	Yellow with golden tones
ideal pairings	Spicy-sweet foods; curry dishes; pasta or seafood with light butter/citrus sauces; roasted white meats; mushrooms and garlic

and everything to do with the body of the wine.

At The Urban Grape, our 5W wines fall into two categories. First, we've got lighter-bodied wines that are influenced by everything a winemaker can do to add body—neutral-barrel fermentation, *battonage* (not just wine sitting on its lees, but having the lees stirred through the wine at regular intervals, sort of like shaking up a snow globe), and barrel aging in new oak for a period of months. Some winemakers even employ maceration—a red-wine technique that utilizes skin contact during fermentation—for varietals like Grüner Veltliner. And don't forget about residual sugar (RS). A little RS left in the wine also boosts body. Winemakers have tricks, and when it comes to fattening up light-bodied wines, they aren't afraid to use them. However, up here, we won't see those ethereally light-bodied grape varietals we learned about in 1W because they're just too delicate to handle these techniques.

Although we've seen them lower down the Progressive Scale, naturally heavier-bodied varietals, like Chardonnay, burst onto the scene in 5W. Unlike what we'll see in later chapters, winemakers are showing real restraint here, and only employing a touch of this or a dash of that to bring out the best aspects of their wine. An easy cheat for this chapter is to remember that winemakers are using either a combination of partial techniques or one full technique. For instance, a winemaker might use a combination of partial malolactic fermentation (ML) and a short time in oak

aging to achieve body. Or full malolactic fermentation, but no oak aging. Or maybe barrel fermentation and some oak aging, but no ML. Like a dash of salt or a grind of pepper, sometimes a little goes a long way. This is what endlessly fascinates us about wine. 5W is a crossroads for white wine, and there are a lot of ways to get here!

GEEKOUT: MALOLACTIC WHAT?!

We can't go any further without understanding malolactic fermentation, or ML. ML is an important winemaking technique for red wine, but it's also vital for richer styled white wines. So what is it?

At the end of primary fermentation, wine has malic acid in it, making it taste naturally tart, like a granny smith apple. For some white wines, this is a desired trait, and the story is done. For others, the wine goes through a secondary fermentation, and malic acid is converted to lactic acid, the same acid in milk and dairy products. The purpose is to calm the tart acidity of wine, and impart a softer and rounder mouthfeel. The process of ML always adds body to a wine, which is why winemakers control whether wine goes through partial or full ML depending on their desired end result.

The resulting lactic acid is *the thing* that gives white wine the "buttery" mouthfeel, smell, and flavor, thanks to a resulting chemical called diacetyl. This technique needs to be used judiciously or it will overpower the wine's fruit and acid. Lactic acid gives wine more body, and also helps it stand up to creamier food pairings. ML may be used sparingly in 5W, but by 8W it's full speed ahead.

Fun fact: You need warmth for ML to occur, and some cellars in regions like Burgundy simply never get warm enough. Hence, they use other techniques to impart body.

Our Favorite Regions and Varietals

We have to start, yet again, in France. Yes, we keep returning there, but that's not *just* because we have a love for French wine. The country has an incredible array of winemaking regions and, more often than not, their wines are the standard against which all others are judged. It's also the original home to the most popular varietals grown throughout the world. There's just no escaping France!

FRANCE

REGION: Bordeaux
VARIETAL: Semillon, Sauvignon Blanc

White Bordeaux receives little of the fanfare of red Bordeaux. We think this is because it's hard to keep the sub-regions of Bordeaux straight and people have a pre-conceived notion that it is expensive. Let's face it, Bordeaux is intimidating and it's easier for customers to keep moving. We beg you to give it a chance. White Bordeaux, most often a blend of Sauvignon Blanc and Semillon, is usually less about aromatics and more about texture. The best examples have a natural waxiness that coats your tongue and provides a nice palate for food. We gravitate toward wines from Graves, the most famous appellation, and Pessac-Léognan, which we believe produces the best White Bordeaux.

FRANCE

REGION: Languedoc-Roussillon
VARIETAL: Grenache Blanc, Marsanne

The Languedoc-Roussillon region in France is the largest winemaking region in the world, covering the entire Mediterranean coastline of France from Spain to Provence. Because of its size, smaller sub-regions are being created in an attempt to more accurately reflect the different terroirs of the region. One of those is the newly created Languedoc-Roussillon-Midi-Pyrénées, influenced by the Mediterranean on one side and the Pyrenees Mountains on the other. We're in love with the region's medium-bodied, blended white wines, typically made from Marsanne, Roussanne, Clairette, Grenache Blanc, Muscat, and other regional varietals. Expect a desperately needed name change for this region in the near future, and then keep your eye on their affordable, intriguing wines.

ITALY

REGION: Le Marche
VARIETAL: Verdicchio

Le Marche is one of Italy's most under-rated wine regions, most likely because it focuses on white wine and stays largely clear of the most serious red wine grapes. It's best known for growing the Verdicchio grape, and no DOC does it better than Castelli di Jesi. Maritime influences abound from both the Adriatic and two nearby Italian rivers, as do mineral deposits in the soil. The Verdicchio from Jesi is round and soft, with its characteristic green notes and mineral-driven acidity throughout.

WHAT TO EAT WITH
— 5W WINES —

The 5W wines come from all over the world and many different types of climates, and also exhibit a range of production techniques. They are generally lower in acid than their predecessors on the Progressive Scale, but haven't gotten overly creamy because there is not yet much malolactic fermentation being applied. Therefore, they're very mellow pairing agents that taste great with a wide variety of food.

THAI NIGHT IS THE BEST NIGHT

Whether we're making it at home or ordering take-out, Thai-inspired curry dishes are a staple at our house. The cuisine can be hard to pair to because any good Thai dish has lots of diverging elements: salt, spice, freshness, and creaminess. Luckily, the wines in 5W are a bit of a mixed bag as well, making it easier to find a wine that fits your palate and the demands of a Thai dish. No matter what 5W wine you pick, the body of the wine is going to be a perfect match for the weight and flavor of a curry dish.

There are plenty of options, from a heavier, oak-aged Sauvignon Blanc to a lighter, European-style Chardonnay in this section. All will taste great with Thai food. But the star of the group will always be an off-dry Riesling. Riesling and Thai cuisine almost always work together to create a magical tasting moment.

We make easy at-home curry dishes all the time, even for lunch! Simply melt 1 tablespoon of coconut oil in a sauté pan, and add red or green curry paste to taste (I use about 2-3 tablespoons). Let the paste cook for about 30 seconds, and then add in a can of coconut milk. Whisk to combine, and add chopped vegetables and shredded chicken, if desired. Simmer until tender and serve over rice. Top with coconut flakes, nuts, and chopped cilantro.

PERFECT PAIRINGS

Spicy-sweet foods

Curry dishes

Pasta with light butter/ citrus sauce

Lightly creamy dishes, especially seafood

Roasted white meats

Mushrooms, garlic

FOODS TO AVOID

Heavy braises

ONE TO TRY

ONE TO TRY

BADENHORST FAMILY WINERY "SECATEURS" CHENIN BLANC (SWARTLAND, SOUTH AFRICA)

A TWO-WEEK HONEYMOON IN SOUTH Africa fostered our lifelong love affair with the country, its people, and its varied winemaking regions. We knew the book needed a South African wine in it as an homage to this trip, and the producer was an obvious choice: Badenhorst Family Wines.

Badenhorst is owned by two cousins, Adi and Hein Badenhorst, whose fathers were both winemakers before them. Adi has visited The Urban Grape, and he is a trip. Funny, vivacious, and gracious, his wines are a reflection of his passionate outlook on life.

The majority of the grapes used by Badenhorst are biodynamically grown on their farm in the Swartland appellation. They've lovingly restored a farmhouse, production facility, and cellar, as well as revitalized the abandoned bush vines on the surrounding property. The vines are old—planted in the 1950s and '60s—the soil is granite, and the vineyards aren't irrigated. Those three elements add up to stressed-out grapes that produce low yields of concentrated, flavorful juice that needs little more than a watchful eye from Adi.

The winery has two labels, the higher-end AA Badenhorst, and the reasonably priced Secateurs. The Secateurs Chenin Blanc is all that is good and right about Chenin in one memorable bottle. The grapes are left In clusters and whole-fruit fermented, stems and all, in concrete tanks and old oak casks. Neither of these vessels impart anything into the wine that would overpower its natural beauty. After fermentation, the wine is left on its lees, with occasional stirring, for seven months. And that's it! A traditionally made wine that kind of makes itself. In fact, Badenhorst Family Winery has started producing beer to keep busy during the months when the wine is just doing its thing.

If you take anything from our spotlight on Badenhorst let it be this: Simple wine, made in a simple way by passionate people, can produce affordable bottles of pure wine genius. And, it pairs well with almost everything!

LET'S PAIR IT
Grilled Shrimp with Pistachio Romesco

The Badenhorst Chenin Blanc is one of those wines that tastes great with absolutely everything—we could have paired it with half the recipes in this book! **But without a doubt the best food pairing we found for this South African wine was Gabriel's Grilled Shrimp with Pistachio Romesco.** The pairing is effortless. The wine naturally has some chewy tannic structure, which is a home run with the similarly chewy, medium-bodied texture of the shrimp. The nose of the wine has a sourdough bread aroma, which really comes alive against the lush yeastiness of the Romesco sauce. Both the wine and the shrimp are crowd-pleasers. Chill down the wine and then double, triple, even quadruple the recipe for an instant cocktail party.

GRILLED SHRIMP
with **PISTACHIO ROMESCO**

SERVES 4
AS AN APPETIZER

GRILLED SHRIMP

1 pound shrimp, peeled
and deveined

8 to 10 wooden/bamboo
skewers, soaked in water
for at least an hour (or metal
skewers, if you fancy)

1 garlic clove

1 lemon

1 tablespoon fresh
thyme leaves

¼ teaspoon red
pepper flakes

3 tablespoons extra virgin
olive oil

Kosher salt and freshly
ground black pepper

Vegetable oil

1 tablespoon sliced chives

Pistachio Romesco
(recipe below)

PISTACHIO ROMESCO

½ cup extra virgin olive
oil, divided

½ cup ciabatta or French
bread, cut into cubes

1 medium onion, sliced

2 garlic cloves, sliced

1 roasted yellow pepper
(jarred or fresh with
skin removed)

¼ cup shelled,
toasted pistachios

1 teaspoon salt

½ teaspoon paprika

¼ teaspoon red
pepper flakes

1 tablespoon freshly
squeezed lemon juice

2 dashes sherry vinegar

¼ cup fresh Italian
parsley, chopped

¼ cup water

This is a very versatile entertaining recipe. By adding some greens, this could easily become an entrée; plated singularly, it is a perfect hors d'oeuvre. As it's pictured, this dish can go really fancy if you find head-on prawns. But for a simpler presentation and preparation, use fresh, wild American shrimp— preferably, that hasn't been frozen. —GABRIEL

In groups of three or four, skewer the shrimp, running a skewer straight though the midpoint of each shrimp. (It should look like the shrimp are spooning.) Lay skewers down flat in a large baking dish.

In a small bowl, use a Microplane or the finest side of a box grater, to grate the garlic. Repeat the process with the lemon, taking care to grate only the very outside of the lemon; cut the lemon in half and set aside. Add the thyme leaves and the red pepper flakes. Drizzle about 3 tablespoons olive oil into the bowl and stir to combine. Brush the marinade mixture over the shrimp, and then turn the skewers over so that the marinade side is face down. Let sit for 15 minutes or refrigerate for up to 12 hours before cooking.

Fifteen minutes before you intend to cook the shrimp, preheat the grill to high. When the grill is ready, season the shrimp with salt and pepper. Turn the flame to low and brush the grill grates with the vegetable oil. Lay the skewers on the grates diagonally (this will make it easier to peel them off the grates). Cover and cook for 60 to 90 seconds, and then flip the skewers. Cook for another 60 to 90 seconds; remove when the shrimp feel firm and are no longer translucent. Transfer to a serving plate, and remove the skewers. Drizzle the shrimp with more olive oil and a squeeze of the reserved lemon; sprinkle with chives. Spread Pistachio Romesco on individual plates and place 2 to 3 shrimp over top.

PISTACHIO ROMESCO

This recipe calls for roasted yellow peppers, which you can find jarred at the grocery store—but by all means, if you know how, I definitely recommend roasting your own.

In a large, high-sided sauté pan, heat ¼ cup of the olive oil over medium heat. Add the bread to the oil and fry until golden, about 3 to 4 minutes. Remove the bread from the pan, and turn the heat to low. Add the onions and garlic to the pan and cook until they are translucent and just starting to color, about 4 to 5 minutes. Remove from the heat and spoon the onion and garlic into the bowl of a food processor along with the roasted pepper, pistachios, and bread. Blend the ingredients until they begin to

form a paste; scrape down the side of the bowl. Pulse and scrape the sides down again. Drizzle in the remaining olive oil and add the salt, paprika, red pepper flakes, lemon juice, a dash or two of sherry vinegar to taste, and the chopped parsley. Pulse briefly. Add the water, a small amount at a time, pulsing after each addition until you reach your desired consistency. Adjust seasonings as needed.

THE HOME OF THE RHÔNE

6W IS OUR FIRST REAL STOP INTO THE world of truly warm-climate wines. These wines are comprised of grapes that are grown in warmer temperatures, where there is generally more sunshine. The grapes themselves typically have thicker skins, and develop more sugar during the longer ripening seasons. As a result of the higher sugars, the fermented grapes produce wines with more alcohol than we saw at the beginning of the Progressive Scale. All of this adds up to wines with more body and texture.

While we don't organize our wines by varietal at the store, we do have areas where grapes naturally cluster together

AT A GLANCE

climate	Increased warmth and sunshine; some Mediterranean-style climates
regions	Rhône Valley and Burgundy, France; Sicily, Italy; Goriska Brda, Slovenia; Mosel, Germany
varietals	Grenache Blanc, Marsanne, Roussanne, Viognier, Chardonnay, Carricante, Catarratto, Ribolla Gialla, Riesling
technique	A mix of winemaker techniques including partial malolactic fermentation and oak aging
characteristics	Integrated acidity and minerality with a creamy texture and a mouthfeel of whole milk
color	More golden-hued than yellow
ideal pairings	Creamy dishes with citrus notes; root vegetables; veal; oil, butter, and jus sauces; chilled fish salads

and dominate a section. This happens in 6W, where Rhône varietals rule the wall. These historic grapes, which were first grown in the Rhône Valley of France, are a vital segment of the wine world, and produce some of the most pleasing white wines on the market. Despite their roots in the Rhône Valley, Rhône varietals are now found outside of France, with particular popularity in Santa Barbara County, California, due to its similarly long and warm growing season.

There are lots of white Rhône varietals, but the major players at The Urban Grape are Grenache Blanc, Marsanne, Roussanne, and Viognier. Grenache Blanc is higher in alcohol than the other grapes, and brings green apple acidity to the wines. Roussanne is also known for its bright acid, while savory Marsanne has incredible fruit flavors of ripe melon and honey. Viognier is the most temperamental of the lot, and very low in acid. But its aromatics are stop-the-presses magical. The different varietals, particularly Marsanne and Roussanne, are often blended together to produce wines with bright acidity, enticing aromatics, and a fruit-driven palate—a perfect trifecta!

In the Rhône Valley, winemakers usually do not let these wines go through malolactic fermentation so that they can preserve their acid and avoid making wines that are flabby and one-dimensional. This is not always the case with American winemakers, who like to treat these wines more like Chardonnay, and put them through ML and age them in new oak. When it comes to Grenache Blanc, Marsanne, and Roussanne, our palates prefer to stay in France. But Viognier, which

is grown up and down the West Coast, from Southern California to Washington State, benefits from the Pacific's coastal influences. The result is that Viognier, often a blending grape in France, shines on its own in the hands of American winemakers. (We'll have more to say about that in the next chapter.)

GEEKOUT: CORKED WINE

It happens to all of us: You uncork a bottle of wine and are greeted by aromas of swampy basement, wet dog, and decomposing cardboard. Delicious? No, definitely, not. What in the world is going on?

Cork is a living compound made from the cork oak tree, and is susceptible to a fungus that causes a chemical reaction when it comes into contact with chloride left over from bottle, and bottle-line, sanitization. The result is labeled 2-4-6 Trichloroanisole, or TCA. TCA is wine's sworn enemy—it robs your bottle of fruit aromas and flavors and replaces them with the aforementioned dankness. This wine is bad. You should not drink this wine.

For reasons we cannot understand, corked wine is the dirty secret of the wine world. People, even sommeliers, love to downplay its existence. We think this is because some people are more sensitive to TCA than others, and a wine expert can get embarrassed if he or she has missed the cork taint. But here is the reality: If a wine is corked, always ask for another bottle. You are not judging the wine seller, sommelier, winemaker, or even the wine itself. Most good wine stores will happily replace the bottle for you. If not, you may unfairly critique a varietal or region as being dank, and we'd never want that! The moral of this story? If it's corked, send it back.

Our Favorite Regions and Varietals

French Rhônes rule the roost, but that doesn't mean there are not options outside of France. 6W wines are grown in regions from Southern California to Australia. Like a good travel agent, we promote visiting as many countries as possible in your lifetime. It's just that our preferred mode of transportation is the wine glass.

FRANCE

REGION: Rhône Valley
VARIETAL: Grenache Blanc

Before we bounce out of the Rhône Valley, let's visit the Lirac AOC in the Rhône, the appellation directly across the river from its more well-known neighbor, Châteauneuf-du-Pape (CNP). Like CNP, Lirac has flat vineyards that allow its grapes to be brutalized by the forceful Mistral winds that come ripping through the valley at gale force speed. The vines grow low to the ground in response, but the grapes lose moisture from the winds. The result is a higher concentration of flavor, and ultimately of the body of the wine. The wines of Lirac, especially the Grenache Blanc, are still growing in popularity but are well worth seeking out. If you can't find them, reach for an easier-to-find and just as delightful Châteauneuf-du-Pape Blanc.

SLOVENIA

REGION: Goriska Brda
VARIETAL: Ribolla Gialla

The former Yugoslavian republics are the oldest winemaking regions in the world, with evidence of winemaking dating back to 5th century BC. Slovenia was the first former republic to bounce back after the Yugoslav war, and recently their wines have been finding fans throughout the United States. It can still be hard to find Slovenian wine stateside, but the easiest to locate are from a region called Goriska Brda, an area with both alpine and Mediterranean influences. Geographically, the region actually straddles both Slovenia and Collio, Italy, and both countries make fantastic Ribolla Gialla wines. A Slovenian tradition of making white wines with some skin contact adds body and texture to these intriguing wines.

GERMANY

REGION: Mosel
VARIETAL: Riesling

Mosel, Germany, is a long narrow region on the Western border that would touch France, if not for the tiny country of Luxembourg. Its steep slopes are nearly impossible to farm, and the region itself is barely warm enough to grow its flagship grape, Riesling. The grapes are dependent on the reflection of the sun coming off of the Mosel, Saar, and Ruwer rivers to increase the amount of warmth to a viable level. Caring for and harvesting the grapes can be so difficult here—it's a wonder people continue to cultivate vines at all. But thank goodness they do. Laser sharp, with lemon acidity, and never-ending brightness on the finish, these wines are intriguingly medium-bodied, making them an exquisite pairing for almost any meal.

WHAT TO EAT WITH
— 6W WINES —

An increase in warmth, sun, and a strong influence of Mediterranean-style climate means that we're seeing wines with increased body, texture, and fruitiness. We're starting to see malolactic fermentation in the 6W wines, even if it's only partial ML. Though these wines are getting creamier, a refreshing acidity and minerality appear throughout.

NIKKI CHICKIE MILANESE

Boneless, skinless chicken breasts, sliced in half length-wise

Salt and pepper

Flour

Eggs

Panko breadcrumbs

Dried basil and oregano

Grated Parmesan cheese

Oil (avocado, coconut, canola, olive, we've tried them all)

Cherry tomatoes

Arugula

My mom, sister-in-law, and I all make a mean chicken cutlet, but it was my sister-in-law, Nikki, who started calling the cutlets "Nikki Chickie." The name stuck. These are versatile, but our favorite way to serve them is as a Milanese salad, with leftovers stuck into buns and made into easy chicken parm sammies the next day.

Line the sliced chicken breasts up on a cutting board. Season generously with salt and pepper. Line up three pie plates and fill the first with flour, the second with beaten eggs mixed with a dash of water, and the third with the panko mixed with herbs and grated cheese. Dredge the chicken in the flour, then eggs, then panko and place them on a second cutting board. Meanwhile, heat oil (I love avocado oil, but I've made them in every kind of oil) in a cast iron skillet. The oil should come half way up the cutlet. Working in batches, fry the cutlets for about four minutes per side, until they are nice and brown all over. Move to a paper towel. Replace lost oil before each batch.

Serve chicken over arugula dressed in a simple lemon vinaigrette. Top with halved cherry tomatoes that have been mixed with minced garlic (I use an unholy amount), olive oil, salt, and pepper. Sometimes I add slices of Parmesan, some capers or olives, and parsley as well. Use your imagination for the topping.

PERFECT PAIRINGS

Creamy dishes, with citrus

Root vegetables

Oil, butter, jus sauces

Chilled fish salads

Veal

Neutral herbs and spices

FOODS TO AVOID

Spicy foods

ONE TO TRY

DOMAINE J.A. FERRET POUILLY-FUISSÉ (BURGUNDY, FRANCE)

KEEPING THE SUB-REGIONS AND appellations of French growing regions straight can be nearly impossible, even for those who taste wine for a living. This confusion often intimidates people from exploring Burgundy, a world-renowned region that boasts five sub-regions (six if you count Beaujolais, a discussion we'll have in the red wine chapters), and countless appellations, that are known for producing different styles of Pinot Noir and Chardonnay, as well as some Gamay and Aligote. An undeniable fan favorite is Pouilly-Fuissé, one of the Southern-most appellations in Burgundy, located in the sub-region known as the Mâconnais.

Pouilly-Fuissé is known for having complex soils comprised of everything from silt to clay to limestone to alluvium. It's also known for amphitheater-style vineyards that ring the towns, creating a breathtaking view, showcasing man and nature in perfect harmony. But at Domaine J.A. Ferret, it's woman and nature that have been in perfect harmony, ever since the estate's inception in 1840.

In a country historically dominated by male winemakers, the fact that Ferret has only had female winemakers for its 176-year history is absolutely unheard of. Not only did women oversee the production of the wine, but Jeanne Ferret changed the region for the better when she rebounded from World War II and became the first domaine in the region to utilize estate vinification—meaning, she left the grape co-op system that had ensured survival during both world wars, but also had devastating effects on the region's quality. Instead, she struck out on her own, took control, and began producing high-quality, single vineyard estate bottlings. In time, Domaine J.A. Ferret became the most highly regarded producer in the region—and may have saved Pouilly-Fuissé in the process.

When Jeanne's daughter, Colette, saw that there would be no heir for the estate, she made sure to leave it in good hands by selling it to Louis Jadot, a world-famous wine company. They installed Audrey Braccini, a caring and intuitive winemaker, who has carried on the woman-winemaking tradition left by the Ferret family with pride and integrity. Her wines embody the best of the region: brightly acidic and mineral-driven Chardonnays that perfectly embody the best characteristics of Pouilly-Fuissé.

LET'S PAIR IT

Black Bass with Red Onions, Rye Croutons, and Olive Tapenade

The Ferret Chardonnay is an intriguing wine. It tastes wonderful on its own, but when paired with a meal that has some meatiness and fat to it, the wine comes alive. On the flip side, because it is more delicate than its California counterparts, we needed to find a recipe that wouldn't overpower its pretty lemon-lime acidity. **Luckily, this Black bass with Olive Tapenade recipe proved to be an ideal pairing for our French Chardonnay.** Much like the wine, black bass is firm but lean. The dish as a whole is at times brightly acidic, fleshy and meaty, earthy and green, and piquantly pickled. When paired with the Ferret, all of these experiences are mirrored in the glass.

BLACK BASS

with RED ONIONS, RYE CROUTONS, AND OLIVE TAPENADE

SERVES 4

BLACK BASS, RED ONIONS, AND RYE CROUTONS

4 tablespoons butter, divided

2 slices rye bread, crusted, and cut into small, even dice

2 tablespoons extra virgin olive oil, divided

1 red onion, thickly sliced

4 slices bacon

1 clove garlic, sliced

½ pound baby spinach, washed

Kosher salt and freshly ground black pepper

Four 6-ounce black bass fillets, trimmed and lightly scored on the skin side

2 tablespoons canola oil

1 teaspoon lemon thyme or regular thyme leaves

1 teaspoon freshly squeezed lemon juice

4 tablespoons Olive Tapenade (recipe below)

OLIVE TAPENADE

3 Meyer lemons, zested and juiced

1 red onion, diced

2 tablespoons honey

1 tablespoon cider vinegar

Sea salt to taste

1 pint pitted Castelveltrano, or other mild green olives

2 tablespoons extra virgin olive oil

2 tablespoons chopped flat-leaf parsley

1 teaspoon sliced chives

There are a few steps to this dish, but the addition of the sautéed onion, croutons, and tapenade add flavor and texture. Of course, if you want to make it really easy, you can simply buy a jar of tapenade. But for those who see the virtue in a challenge, I've included a recipe for one below. —GABRIEL

Preheat oven to 350°F. Prepare a small sheet pan by rubbing it with 1 tablespoon butter.

Melt 1 tablespoon of butter over low heat. In a medium bowl, toss melted butter with rye croutons, then transfer to prepared sheet pan. Bake in the oven for 7 to 8 minutes, or until golden brown. Remove from heat and reserve.

Heat a large sauté pan over medium-high heat and add olive oil. Lay slices of red onion in the pan and cook for 3 to 4 minutes per side, or until they start to soften and develop a slight char. Season onions with salt, remove them from the pan and set aside.

Wipe the sauté pan clean and place back over medium-high heat. Cook the bacon until rendered and crisp. Remove from the pan and let cool slightly, then crumble and set aside. Remove excess bacon fat from the pan and wipe clean. Combine 1 tablespoon of olive oil and garlic in the same pan and place over medium heat. Once the garlic starts to turn golden, about 1 to 2 minutes, add the spinach, season with salt and pepper, and then cover the pan for 30 seconds. Remove the lid, and with a pair of tongs turn the spinach over a few times. Turn the burner off before the spinach is completely wilted, and then add the red onions and bacon and toss with tongs to combine. Season to taste and let sit at room temperature until ready to serve.

Pat the bass fillets dry with a paper towel. Season both sides with salt and pepper. Place a large, cast iron sauté pan over high heat. Once the pan is hot, add the canola oil, then lay the fillets in the pan skin side down, making sure that they are pressed firmly against the pan. Turn the heat down to medium, and let the fish cook, undisturbed for about 4 to 5 minutes, until the edges appear deeply golden. Turn off the heat, but leave the pan on the burner. Add the remaining 2 tablespoons butter and thyme to the pan. Gently flip the fillets over in the pan. Add the lemon juice, then pick up and swirl the pan to coat the fish with the butter and

lemon sauce. Remove the fish from the pan and plate each individual fillet with the spinach. Top the fish with the Olive Tapenade and garnish with croutons.

OLIVE TAPENADE

In a medium bowl, combine the Meyer lemon juice and zest, red onion, honey, cider vinegar, and a sprinkling of salt. Set aside for a few minutes.

Dice the olives and add them to the red onion mixture. Add the olive oil and the herbs. Check the seasoning and adjust if necessary. Set aside until ready to use.

WHERE OLD MEETS NEW

IT'S A GENERALIZATION, BUT A TRUTH, to say that New World winemakers approach winemaking in a different way than do Old World winemakers. Old World wines (most easily defined as "The Settlers," or European countries like France, Italy, Spain, and the first wine regions, like Slovenia) are more strictly regulated than New World wines (most easily defined as "The Settlees," or the Americas, Australia, South Africa). Producing wines that recall hundreds of years of winemaking tradition is a keystone

climate	Warmer Old and New World regions with abundant sunshine
regions	Rioja, Spain; Santa Barbara County, San Luis Obispo County, and Sonoma, California; Burgundy, Alsace, and Loire Valley, France
varietals	Viura, Chardonnay, Gewürztraminer, Chenin Blanc, Grenache Blanc, Marsanne, Roussanne, Viognier
technique	Partial or full malolactic fermentation with a mix of new- and old-oak aging
characteristics	Ripe fruit, softer texture, and fuller body with a mouthfeel like half-and-half; mineral-driven with acid present
color	Bright, golden hues
ideal pairings	Game meats; earthy vegetables; firmer, lower acidity cheese; cream sauces over white meats and veal

to Old World winemaking, whereas New World winemakers have more freedom to play around with the end result.

But like a Venn diagram, the two shall overlap at some point. In the world of white wine, 7W is where Old World and New World whites meet, imitate, and flatter one another for one brief, shining moment. And in no varietal is this more obvious than Chardonnay.

Here, we find the heaviest-bodied of the white Burgundies, from regions like Côtes de Beaune and Côtes de Nuits. But we also find cooler-climate American Chardonnay from California's Sonoma Coast and Santa Rita Hills, as well as Willamette Valley, Oregon. These are the regions that are farming higher-elevation "mountain" fruit that cannot ripen as richly as it can on the valley floor.

In most cases, these New World Chardonnays are being made in an Old World manner, with the belief that imitation is the sincerest form of flattery. Some Burgundy winemakers have even struck out to find their fortunes in the New World, and are producing wines that remind them of home. Both sets of winemakers are throwing just about everything at their Chardonnay— partial ML, barrel fermentation, lees contact, concrete egg aging—but are stopping short of full malolactic fermentation and new oak aging.

There are two distinct sets of Chardonnay lovers in the world: those who love the Old World, restrained-style, and those who prefer the big, bold, buttery flavors and body of American Chardonnay. 7W is where you can find the bottles that make both sides happy, which, in our family at least, has saved many a dinner party.

GEEKOUT:
PLACE BEFORE GRAPE

What makes you, you? Is it what's inside of you, or where you're from? The answer is very different when discussing Old World and New World wine labels. Old World wine regions are heavily regulated, and only allowed to grow specified grape varietals for each appellation. For example, the region of Burgundy is only allowed to grow the white varietals of Chardonnay, Aligote, Pinot Gris, and Pinot Blanc, of which Chardonnay is the majority. The wine buyer is supposed to know these regional distinctions, and be able to judge what grape is in the bottle solely based on knowing the region. That's why a Chardonnay from Chablis, Burgundy is simply called "a Chablis," and not a "Chardonnay." It's clear for those who grew up with this system. But it can be seriously confusing for Americans.

In the Wild Wild West (aka: the New World), some grapes may do better than others in certain regions, but we don't have laws that define what winemakers can grow. Therefore, our labels focus on the grape varietal before the region, like a Chardonnay from the Sonoma Coast. In general, Americans prefer to shop by grape over region.

If only we had a nickel for every time we heard, "Oh no, I don't like Chardonnay at all, my favorite wine is Chablis!" But, now you know—and wine knowledge is wine power!

Our Favorite Regions and Varietals

If 7W is a tale of two Chardonnays, then we would be remiss not to look at two Chardonnay producing countries in more depth here. People who are dedicated to California Chardonnay have trouble believing that they could ever love a French Chardonnay (and vice versa), but we believe there is harmony to be found.

FRANCE

REGION: Loire Valley
VARIETAL: Chenin Blanc

Outside of French Chardonnay, we are evermore obsessed with Chenin Blanc from the Loire Valley region of Vouvray. Vouvray produces dry, off-dry, sweet, and sparkling wines, and it is the sweet, or "Moelleux," Vouvray that we're focusing on in 7W—the only truly sweet wine we're profiling in the book. The grapes used to make "Moelleux" Vouvray have "noble rot," a fungus whose official name is Botrytis cinerea. This fungus causes the grapes to shrivel, thereby intensifying the sugars and flavors in the juice. Despite being sweet, the best "Moelleux" wines maintain a dry finish. They age incredibly well (we're talking decades), and develop additional nuances with time. This is not an everyday wine, but worth seeking out to pair with creamy, salty dishes.

FRANCE

REGION: Burgundy
VARIETAL: Chardonnay

Let's start with the grandfather of Chardonnay, the Burgundy wine region, and specifically for 7W, the Puligny-Montrachet appellation. Burgundy has white wines that range from 4W to 8W, with each appellation known for a slightly different body of the wine. Puligny-Montrachet produces one of the heaviest bodied Chardonnays in Burgundy. As they are throughout Burgundy, the wines are influenced heavily by minerality, but these Chardonnays have a creamy, lactose quality, as well as nuances of lime and honey. Despite being full-bodied, there is a tension to them that makes the wine almost spring out of the glass. They age well, and are particularly well matched to foie gras.

UNITED STATES

REGION: San Luis Obispo County, California
VARIETAL: Chardonnay

Edna Valley in California's San Luis Obispo County boasts the longest growing season in the world, with bud break in February and harvest in October. The grapes mature slowly, soaking up the sun, while being cooled by the fog and breezes coming off of the Pacific Ocean. All the while they are pulling up minerals from the rich, volcanic soil. The Chardonnays from this region usually see barrel fermentation, full malolactic fermentation, and aging in French oak barrels. The result is a mineral-driven tension to the wine, a creamy, lactose quality, vibrant lime acidity, and honey overtones. (Sound familiar?)

WHAT TO EAT WITH
— 7W WINES —

As we move into the relatively warmer climates of the Old and New World, *we can finally start to fatten up our recipes with heavier meats, sauces, and vegetables. Flavors can become bolder and dishes can contain more richness. There is an element of seasonality that comes into play as well. Even though any wine can taste great on any day, these fuller-bodied wines come alive with fall flavors.*

BAY SCALLOPS WITH ROOT VEGETABLES

Carrots and parsnips

Whole milk, warmed

Bay scallops

Butter

Lemon

Sliced grapes

Thanksgiving is our favorite meal of the year, and while these wines go well with Thanksgiving dinner, there is another seasonal pairing that we like even more. Atlantic Bay Scallops are a sweet coastal delicacy with a short harvest season. Inspired by a recipe from the book *Vineyard Harvest,* by Tina Miller, we serve our scallops over pureed root vegetables and finish them with a lemon sauce and sliced grapes. This buttery, sweet, yet lemony dish is perfectly mirrored in the 7W wines, which are themselves buttery, with sweet tropical fruit, and bright acidity.

First, boil large chunks of carrot and parsnip in water. When they are soft, puree them with a little warm milk and a tablespoon of butter until you've achieved a silky mashed consistency. Season with salt and pepper. Then, fire up a cast iron skillet until it's good and hot. Add vegetable oil to just coat the pan, and add the scallops. (Make sure they're washed, dried, and the little foot removed). Season the scallops and let them sit until they are mostly cooked through and seared on the bottom. Then, flip them and let sit until just cooked through. Remove them from the skillet. Add a few tablespoons of butter and the juice of a lemon to the pan, scraping up the brown bits. To serve, spoon the puree into a serving bowl, add the scallops and a generous handful of sliced grapes, and spoon the pan sauce over top.

+ PERFECT PAIRINGS

Firmer, lower acidity cheese

·················

Dishes with more viscosity

·················

Game meats

·················

Cream sauces over white meats, veal

·················

Eggplant

⊗ FOODS TO AVOID

Delicate ceviche dishes

ONE TO TRY

GUNDLACH BUNDSCHU WINERY GEWÜRZTRAMINER (SONOMA COAST, CALIFORNIA)

SOMEONE NEEDS TO DEVELOP A miniseries about the saga of the Gundlach and Bundschu families and get it on to TV, pronto. Their 160-year history in Sonoma, California, has all the elements of a juicy docudrama: immigrants working their way up to be pillars of society; the joining of two upwardly mobile families through marriage; the growth of a family business; the utter destruction of the family business not once but *twice* (first with the earthquake of 1906, and then with Prohibition); the sheer determination to persevere despite the odds; the younger generation swooping in with creative ideas and a dogged determination to revive the family name; and ultimately, not just a return to the glory days, but the full realization of the dream that began in 1858. This is Gundlach Bundschu Winery, or as they're known today, Gun Bun.

Although the family continued to grow and sell grapes after Prohibition, winemaking on Gun Bun's Rhinefarm estate was dormant from 1919 until 1976, which is when Jim Bundschu produced three estate grown and bottled wines. Since then, Gundlach Bundschu has grown in both reach and prominence, all while understanding that good wine doesn't need to take itself too seriously. The owners are known for their fun-loving attitudes, their music festivals, and their downright hysterical educational videos. (Just do yourself a favor and Google "A Brief History of Merlot.") When you consider that they're the oldest, continuously farmed, family-owned vineyards in California, their ability to make wine accessible for a new generation seems like an amazing feat of rebirth.

All of Gun Bun's grapes are estate grown in 60 vineyard blocks on their 320-acre farm. They make a little bit of everything: Chardonnay, Pinot Noir, Merlot, Zinfandel, Tempranillo, Cabernet Franc, and, of course, Cabernet Sauvignon. All of these wines are fantastic, but our favorite of the bunch is the Gewürztraminer. Maybe that's because it's the grape that most recalls the family's German heritage, and the original rootstock came over with founder Jacob Gundlach. Maybe it's the fact that their Gewürztraminer is fuller bodied, and yet bone-dry with racy acidity—an American take on a historic grape. Or maybe it's just because it's delicious and seems to pair with whatever food or activity we throw at it, whether it be as an aperitif paired with cheese and charcuterie at a dinner party, or paired with take-out in front of a spicy TV miniseries.

LET'S PAIR IT

Crab Toast with Mango Salad

Traditionally grown in Alsace, France, and throughout Germany, Gewürztraminer seems an odd choice to pair with Indian food, but it's a hit every time. **The Gun Bun Gewürztraminer, with its classic flavors of lychee, candied ginger, and Moroccan spice, is no exception, which is why it pairs so nicely with the following Crab Toast with Mango Salad recipe.** The crab toast and wine are both delicious on their own, but when paired together: BOOM. The flavors come alive with passion and vivacity. The wine also helps cool the spicy overtones of the dish, which keeps you coming back for more.

CRAB TOAST

SERVES 4   *with* **MANGO SALAD**

2 mangoes

Kosher salt

Zest and juice of one lime

1 teaspoon fresh ginger, grated with a Microplane or small holes of box grater

½ teaspoon red pepper flakes

1 teaspoon curry powder

2 tablespoons salted cashews, chopped

1 tablespoons sliced scallion greens

4 English muffins, toasted and buttered

2 tablespoons butter

1 shallot, minced

1 pound fresh Jonah or Peekytoe lump crab meat, picked through

What makes this simple dish work is the surprising brininess of the fresh crabmeat playing against the curry spices in the mango salad. Champagne or Ataulfo mangoes (nature's own burrata) add a nice fragrant note here. I like to cut these into quarters and serve them as bite-sized hors d'oeuvres. If you can't find Jonah or Peekytoe, look for the freshest crabmeat you can find—even canned will do in a pinch, though it will likely require some doctoring (think: more seasoning and acid). For the truly adventurous, English muffins are stunningly easy to make, and the sense of satisfaction I get from pulling homemade muffins off the griddle fills all the nooks and crannies of my little heart. —GABRIEL

Preheat oven to 200°F.

Using a sharp knife, peel the mangoes and cut the two large lobes off the pit; cut around the pit to remove the top and the bottom. Treating the mango halves like an onion, cut them into a large, fairly uniform dice. Do the same with the rest of the mango and put all of the dice in a medium-sized mixing bowl. Lightly season the mango with salt. In order, add the lime juice, zest, ginger, pepper, cashews, and scallion greens. Let ingredients sit without tossing.

Put the toasted, buttered English muffins in the oven and heat for 5 minutes. Meanwhile, in a small pot over very low heat, melt the butter. Add the shallots; the moment they become translucent and aromatic, turn off the heat and add the crabmeat, stirring gently to combine. Remove the muffins from the oven and transfer to a serving plate. Generously spoon warm crabmeat on to the muffins. Quickly toss the mango and other ingredients together, and spoon 1 to 2 tablespoons of mango salad over the crabmeat. Serve as is or cut into smaller portions if making hors d'oeuvres.

EASY TIPS FOR WINE COLLECTING

After we'd been dating a year, TJ and I took a trip to California wine country to do a little exploring, and came home with a suitcase full of wine. It was just after this trip that TJ commandeered a corner of one of our closets and turned it into a "wine cellar" for our California purchases. TJ's commandeering would not end there.

When we moved into our first real house together, he took over one of the coat closets and made it into a wine cellar. I will never forget the day when I came home to find a hole blown through the closet wall—right into our newly renovated powder room. Where once a mirror hung there was now the back end of a compressor unit. I cried, and it got fixed. We were down a coat closet, but TJ and our wine were happy.

Our present home, built in 1860, has the perfect dingy corner for TJ's latest MacGyver'ed wine cellar. Window sealant, piped in cool and humid air, and a thick plastic "door" keep our bottles happy while we wait for the basement's eventual renovation. All of this is to say that you don't need a trophy wine cellar, or even trophy wine, to be a wine collector. With a little innovation, or at least a wine storage unit, you, too, can begin collecting.

How to Get Started

Choose a cool, dark area of your house where you can lay bottles down on their side. Laying the wine on its side keeps the corks from drying out. If no area of your home or apartment fits this bill, consider investing in a refrigerated wine storage unit, like a EuroCave.

Know What to Age

Most wine bought in the United States is consumed within 24 hours, but there are certain wines, like the Bordeaux varietals and blends, and more structured Italian wines, that benefit from being left to age for a few additional years. We also suggest aging "special occasion" wines that can be opened on holidays and anniversaries, and birth year wines for your children. We also store wines we buy while traveling, so we can revisit those special moments at home.

Temperature and Humidity

The easiest way to remember what temperature is best for wine is to learn 45-55-65. Don't let your wine get colder than 45 degrees, or hotter than 65 degrees. 55 degrees is ideal, but fluctuation within those temperature points will not stress your wine too badly, especially if you're only cellaring the bottles for a couple of years. Prime humidity for long-term aging of Bordeaux varietals and other age-worthy wines is 60 to 90 percent so that the cork doesn't dry out. Humidity is less important if you're only aging things for a couple years or less, but avoid storing wine in bone-dry humidity.

Keep it Dark and Calm

Wine likes a dark, predictable, and calm environment (don't store it on the other side of the wall from the washing machine, for instance). Massive temperature and humidity fluctuations are much worse for your wine than storing it consistently at a temperature of 70 degrees.

Drink Your Wine

Aging wine is a fun and slightly addictive past time, but at the end of the day, your wine will bring you the most enjoyment when it's in your glass. So don't forget to drink it!

CHAPTER 4

THE HEAVY WEIGHTS

The Porch Pounders are but a distant dot in our rearview mirror, meaning we've moved from the acid-brightness of lemonade to the lushness of hot chocolate. We're entering the land of the richest, heaviest-bodied white wines available on the market. The varied ends of the spectrum are equally intimidating. Many people don't know when to enjoy full-bodied white wines, or what foods to pair with them. In the right moment, however, these wines are some of the most spectacular food pairing wines available, capable of standing up to dishes that would overpower other white wines. If you can't imagine being wooed to this side of the spectrum, just picture yourself on a snowy night with a rich, pulled pork sandwich and a creamy, full-bodied Chardonnay. That will make you a believer in no time!

DIVERSITY'S LAST STAND

UP TO THIS POINT, EVEN IF WE'VE highlighted certain varietals or regions, each section has showcased an array of wines. 8W is really the last time we will see any diversity in white wines, both geographically and in terms of varietals. Lucky for us, 8W is like the United Nations of heavier-bodied wines. Pretty much everyone is represented and they all put on a good show.

Despite the diversity, a common theme runs through the wines of 8W, which makes it a fun section for wine lovers to

climate	Warm climates with lots of sun and large temperature shifts from day to night (diurnal shift)
regions	Mendoza, Argentina; Paso Robles, Russian River Valley, and Carneros, California; Northern Rhône Valley, France; Columbia Valley and Walla Walla, Washington
varietals	Chardonnay, Grenache Blanc, Marsanne, Roussanne, Viognier
technique	Full malolactic fermentation; oak aging, often in a mix of old and new wood, or just new wood
characteristics	Reminiscent of eggnog in body, creaminess, and the presence of warm, baking spice influence
color	Deep golden hues
ideal pairings	Thanksgiving flavors; stuffed mushrooms; pork chops with herbs and apples; Fall bisque soups; loaded nachos

AT A GLANCE

explore: *sunshine.* Medium-bodied grapes grown in the full sun of warm regions get so fat and laden down with sugars that they bulk up beyond what they're capable of doing in cooler climates. Rich soil also helps to make grapes that are languid and lazy, like perfectly ripe and plump tomatoes that do nothing but bask in the sun of the summer heat.

But after everything we've learned so far, do you really believe that it's just sunshine and soil that make these wines so full-bodied? It's not, you're absolutely right. Let's drop in to Sicily and look at the Grillo grape for a moment. Grown in Sicily's sun-baked soils, Grillo's high sugar content historically made it a perfect grape for producing Marsala wine. Vinified on its own, it produces a medium-bodied wine with lots of fruit and citrus aromas and nutty undertones on the palate. The complaint against medium-bodied Grillo is that it's a little *meh*—not as interesting as other varietals and easy to pass over in favor of other, more exciting, Italian wines.

But, when you find Grillo up here around 8W, it's been barrel-aged. Grillo takes beautifully to barrel aging—after all, it was a grape known for being able to stand up to the fortification and oxidation needed to make Marsala. Barrel aging brings this wine to life and makes it interesting and

nuanced. Sun, soil, aging: It's the trifecta that allows a wide array of grapes to make it to the heavyweights—even those that are soon about to be outpaced by their American compatriots.

GEEKOUT:
BREAKING OUT OF THE RUT

The majority of American wine buyers are stuck in what can only be described as a wine buying rut. This is particularly true of people who shop for wine in grocery stores, where choosing a bottle for dinner is as glamorous as remembering to pick up cereal for breakfast.

If this book can teach you anything, it's that when you *Drink Progressively,* you can train yourself to love, and to seek out, many different types of wine. The ritual of looking for a new and exciting bottle becomes as enticing as hitting up a farmers' market to choose the freshest produce. Pairing wine, however inexpensive, to your meals, however simple, becomes a moment of ritual at the end of the day, signaling a time to take a breath, take a sip, and relax.

There are two keys to breaking out of the wine rut. The most important, no matter where you shop, is to experiment. Unless you're having a party, make mixed cases instead of bringing home 12 bottles of the same wine. You might not love them all, but you'll learn. The second is, whenever possible, enlist the aid of a small, locally owned wine shop with passionate employees who can help to lead your journey. A lifetime of wine exploration will be your reward.

Our Favorite Regions and Varietals

Everyone knows Napa and Burgundy, but part of the charm of getting to know good wine is finding the newest, up-and-coming wine regions. This is easier to do in the New World, where new territories are being conquered, tilled, and put under vine all the time. In the Old World, it is more likely that existing regions are simply being rediscovered.

UNITED STATES

REGION: Paso Robles, California
VARIETAL: Grenache Blanc

Before we started The Urban Grape, TJ went on a trip to Paso Robles, a relatively new AVA in California that sits halfway between Los Angeles and San Francisco. The first time he called home, he described Paso Robles as "a little bit cowboy." And, it is. Free to do their own thing, the winemakers of this region have done some of the craziest things with wine, like blend varietals that have never before been in the same bottle. But the region is also known for its outstanding Rhône-inspired wines, like Grenache Blanc. The diverse soils, long, warm days, and cool nights make the region a happy home away from home for Rhône varietals.

UNITED STATES

REGION: Columbia Valley, Washington
VARIETAL: Viognier

Columbia Valley in Washington State has been an AVA since 1984, and has been steadily gaining popularity ever since. The region covers nearly one-third of the state, and nearly all of the grapes grown in Washington come from this AVA. Although the region has many microclimates, the weather is amazingly consistent year after year, so Washington wines are known for having continuity between vintages. There are many sub-appellations within Columbia Valley, with Walla Walla, Yakima Valley, and Wahluke Slope among our favorites and the easiest to find. They all make excellent heavier-bodied white wines, like Viognier.

ARGENTINA

REGION: Mendoza
VARIETAL: Chardonnay

Argentina isn't a new winemaking country, but to many Americans, it seemed like it was when Argentinian Malbec exploded onto the scene a decade ago. In fact, regions throughout the country have been producing wine since the 1800s with great success. The most successful region is Mendoza, where approximately two-thirds of the country's wine is produced. The region's diverse landscape means that there are vineyards planted in both arid deserts and among the highest elevations in the world—which is why the producers are forced to keep things simple and high quality. Their preferred white wine is Chardonnay, which ripens beautifully with such proximity to the sun, but maintains its acidity thanks to cooler temps. If you're sick of paying for Napa and Burgundian Chardonnay, look to Mendoza to ease the strain on your wallet.

WHAT TO EAT WITH
— 8W WINES —

Our wines are moving into a full-bodied expression, and while some people find pairing white wine with so much body challenging, we beg to differ. Delicious with a wide range of foods that often might be paired to red, these wines have enough texture to stand up to traditional comfort meals. There's a baking spice quality to these wines, which makes them wonderful with richer foods.

CLASSIC ROAST CHICKEN AND VEGGIES WITH A TWIST

Ina Garten's Roasted Chicken Recipe

Uniformly chopped root vegetables – carrots, parsnips, turnips, potatoes, sweet potatoes, etc.

Spanish onion, halved and sliced into quarters

Winter greens, such as kale, or any lettuce you prefer

Homemade herbed croutons

Slices of Parmesan cheese

Bacon crumbles

Lemon-Dijon vinaigrette

We could pretend that we have an amazing new way to roast a chicken, but the fact is, Ina Garten's Perfect Roast Chicken recipe is just that: perfect. Stuffed with thyme, garlic, and lemon and roasted for an hour and a half at 425°F, this chicken is tender on the inside, yet covered with crispy skin. What we change up is the way we serve it—over a richly flavored salad that warms us up even on the chilliest night. This oily, rich, and savory dish finds its match with robust 8W wines that can stand up to all of that intensity. Their backbone of acidity brightens the experience. An 8W from any region will work, as this universally adored method for chicken is practiced around the world.

Roast the chicken over a bed of root vegetables and onions. (If I'm feeling flush with time I'll use Gabriel's recipe, page 111, to brine the bird first.) Remove the bird when it's done, stir the veggies in all the fat and chicken juice, and pop them back into the oven until they are perfectly roasted.

Build a salad made of winter greens, the roasted vegetables, croutons, cheese, and bacon crumbles. Top with slices of the chicken. Dress with a lemon-Dijon vinaigrette (lemon, olive oil, garlic or shallot, Dijon mustard, honey or maple syrup, and salt and pepper). I prefer to use stone-ground Dijon mustard, as it adds additional texture to the meal.

PERFECT PAIRINGS

Pork chops with savory herbs and apples

·················

Fall bisque soups

·················

Loaded nachos

·················

Stuffed mushrooms

·················

Thanksgiving flavors

FOODS TO AVOID

Delicate green herbs like cilantro and basil

ONE TO TRY

PEAY VINEYARDS SONOMA COAST CHARDONNAY (SONOMA COAST, CALIFORNIA)

THERE IS SO MUCH TO LOVE ABOUT Peay Vineyards, even before you try the wine. First, there are the people. Husband-and-wife team Nick Peay and Vanessa Wong joined up with brother Andy Peay to embark on what they call their "empirical adventure." Their zest for purity and excellence in winemaking, along with a touch of "fake it 'til you make it" shines through in all of their wines. Second, they're a little rebellious. All three walked away from parental and societal job expectations to see if they could make a name for themselves in the wine world. (They did.) Lastly, they are adorably geeky and don't hide that fact. We've visited thousands of winery websites in the last several years, and the Peay website is the only one with a near dissertation on cross-sectional wind patterns and the role that air mass plays in wine making. It's endearing, it's educational, and it's so very real.

Their wine is endearing, educational, and real, as well. Their vineyard site, especially the lots they chose for their Chardonnay, is risky in that it is heavily influenced by the maritime winds and fog coming off the Pacific, and many people would have worried that the area is too cool to produce fully ripened grapes. They farmed organically for years, believing it to be the best way to make exceptional wine, but didn't file for certification until they felt confident about the nuances of their tricky vineyards—and that there were plenty of effective organic resources available to them in a pinch. But the team at Peay works with Mother Nature instead of against her, and believes that lower yields and a slower growing season lead to wines that are ultimately balanced between fruit and acidity.

They don't set out to make overly fruity or massively full-bodied wines, because the environment simply doesn't let them.

While Peay focuses mostly on single vineyard wines, their Sonoma Coast Chardonnay is a blend of grapes from their different lots and an expression of the winery as a whole. It's creamy and enveloping, but never flabby, thanks to zesty, citrus acidity and distinct minerality. It tastes more Burgundian than stereotypically Californian—a perfect example of how the pendulum in California wine has swung back toward balance. Rich enough to stand up to creamy foods, but acidic enough to cut through the noise, this is a perfect food wine. There is a lot to love about Peay—and after you try it, you'll be as besotted as we are.

LET'S PAIR IT
Broccoli Rabe and Sausage Pasta

No matter what pair with it, the Peay Chardonnay seems to beg for more flavor. **So we put this California Chardonnay up against Gabriel's spicy, bitter, creamy, and rich Broccoli Rabe and Sausage Pasta, and found a delicious match.** By design, this pairing is comfort food at its best. The wine stands up to the huge flavor of this dish, but also helps cut the richness—you'll find yourself going back for seconds of both wine and food. The Peay beautifully handles the bitterness of the broccoli rabe, and the heat of the chili flakes, so feel free to amp it up.

BROCCOLI RABE AND SAUSAGE PASTA

SERVES 4

16 ounces of penne or orecchiette

2 tablespoons extra virgin olive oil plus more for garnish

12 ounces of chicken sausage, removed from casing (Use spicy; come on! I dare you)

4 cups chopped broccoli rabe, cut in rounds roughly ¼-inch thick

2-4 cups hot water

½ cup grated pecorino, plus more for garnish

When Andrea Solimeo joined our team at Ventuno (then, as chef de cuisine; he's now the chef/owner) I blurted out to him: "I basically always make sausage and rabe pasta and it is my favorite thing and I want to put it on the menu some day." A few days later, Dre served me this dish, and it was then that I knew that we were soul mates (me and the pasta, to be clear). Thanks, Dre.

If you have access to (or enjoy making) fresh pasta, like a strozzapretti, this dish will really be the better for it. But, for a standby weeknight meal, when all you want is a glass of wine, a comforting bowl of pasta, and, well, another glass of wine, there's nothing wrong with using dried pasta—either way, this salty, sweet, spicy dish should up your every-night game.   —*GABRIEL*

Cook pasta until just shy of al dente, according to instructions. Drain and set aside. Place a large sauté pan over high heat. Stir in 2 tablespoons olive oil and add the chicken sausage. Spread the sausage out along the bottom of the pan in a thin, even layer. Let the sausage cook for one or two minutes, until the sausage is well browned, but not burnt. Using a wooden spoon, scrape the sausage off the bottom of the pan and break it up. Let cook another 15 seconds, then add the broccoli rabe, plus 2 cups of water. Add the just-cooked pasta to the pan and cook for another minute; add more water if the pan starts to get dry. Toss the pasta in the pan and add the pecorino a tablespoon at a time, tossing after each addition, until the finished product is well emulsified. Garnish with additional shaved pecorino and a drizzle of olive oil.

WELCOME TO THE NEW WORLD

FROM THIS POINT ON, ALMOST EVERY wine we talk about will be New World in provenance, or made in a New World style, with a just a few exceptions. America, South Africa, and Australia have planted their flags and claimed dominance over this side of the white wine Progressive Scale. If you have an Old World passport, chances are you're not coming up here to visit.

It's really not Europe's fault that they can't participate in these sections. It's purely a matter of weather. New World wines don't fall into the first chapter of the white wine

AT A GLANCE

climate	Warm, even hot, climates with beautiful sunshine and long stretches of ideal farming weather; almost all New World
regions	Hawkes Bay, New Zealand; Napa Valley, Sonoma Valley, and Santa Lucia Highlands, California; Casablanca Valley, Chile; Malgas and Stellenbosch, South Africa
varietals	Chardonnay, Chenin Blanc, Gewürztraminer
technique	Primarily full ML and new-oak aging
characteristics	Creamy and smooth with a lift of acid to avoid being boring
color	Pale amber with golden tones
ideal pairings	BLTs; foie gras; bacon turkey burgers; sole meunière; lobster pizza

section because our wine-growing regions just don't get cold enough. Old World wines don't fall into this last chapter because, except for a few regions, it simply doesn't get warm enough. It's a perfect yin-yang of wine making—and yet another example of how expanding your own personal wine palate allows you to enjoy everyone's regional strengths.

Here's what's happening in 9W: We are in the warmest growing areas, but there's at least one factor that is keeping sugar and ripeness levels somewhat in check. It could be that the grapes are grown at high, or extreme elevations; or perhaps they're grown on the coast and receive some maritime influence. The Santa Cruz mountain region is a perfect example of an area that produces big, huge wines, but not quite the biggest because of geographical factors.

Stainless steel fermentation and concrete egg aging are gone. In their place are oak barrel fermentation and oak aging. But just as geographical factors might help take the edge off, these wines are often aged in French oak instead of American oak. It may not seem like a big difference, but it tempers the weight of the wine just enough.

Don't get us wrong: these wines are *big*— full malolactic fermentation sees to that. Too big, in fact, for those who prefer lighter-bodied wines. But we love them because the best winemakers have been careful not

to obliterate the acid. You know you've got a perfect 9W when what starts out as rich and fat on the front of the palate moves into a moment of bright acidy on the mid-palate. It might only be there for a second, but it's what keeps us intrigued and coming back for more.

GEEKOUT:
THE ART OF THE BARREL

We've spent a lot of time discussing barrels—a technique both embraced and shunned in winemaking. Barrels are so important to the outcome of the wine that we considered dividing the white wines into just two sections: B.O. (Before Oak) and A.O. (After Oak). But we weren't sure we wanted to be that kind of a wine bible.

So, what's the deal? Everything matters with oak: the species, the size of the barrel, the treatment (i.e. charring), and the age of the barrel. Each variation has a different outcome on the wine. French oak is the granddaddy of them all. It's considered the best oak for wine making thanks to a more nuanced influence on the finished product. American oak is really only used by New World and Spanish winemakers and whiskey distillers. It's the most flavor-imparting and expressive. Hungarian oak is gaining in popularity, mostly because French oak has gotten so expensive. All oak barrels are used to round out the wine, smoothing off the edges, and helping the wine to function as a cohesive unit. Too much oak is never a good thing. If your wine tastes woody, like a 2x4, it's either not ready to drink, or not properly made.

No matter what, don't fear oak! It's one of the most historic aspects of winemaking, and makes the flavor of many wines, both red and white, much more enjoyable.

Our Favorite Regions and Varietals

9W wines hail almost entirely from the New World, so what's nice about this section is that the wines come from regions that are not the usual suspects. There's also a level of regional hardship that keeps these wines from becoming overly huge and uninteresting. The most balanced wines have a fantastic winemaker at the helm, as well.

UNITED STATES

REGION: Sonoma County, California
VARIETAL: Chardonnay

While Sonoma Coast wines are generally lighter in body, those from Sonoma Valley tend to be fuller-bodied. We're particularly enamored with Chardonnay from the Russian River Valley (RRV), which comprises more than 40 percent of all the grapes grown in the region. RRV producers try hard to bridge the gap between the more mineral-driven Chardonnays from Burgundy and the in-your-face oaky American style wines. Because of the region's many microclimates, producers like to have vineyards throughout the area, either for blending purposes or to highlight the incredible differences in terroir. In general, Chardonnay from this region is purposefully produced in a rich, full-bodied style, but the climate and geography keep them from becoming overly lush. In our book, these are perfect New World-style American Chardonnays.

NEW ZEALAND

REGION: Hawkes Bay
VARIETAL: Chardonnay

The Pacific Ocean is a major factor on California's wine regions, and its influence is also felt outside of California. The North Island of New Zealand is home to Hawkes Bay, the oldest winemaking region in the country. With all that sun, it's easy for this region in New Zealand to make wines that are rich and full-bodied, but the Chardonnay that is grown on the coastline is undeniably influenced by the cooling breezes of the Pacific Ocean. The diverse soils also help to impart interesting nuances to the wine. The wines are huge, but they're interesting, and it's definitely worth exploring Chardonnay from this region.

SOUTH AFRICA

REGION: Malgas
VARIETAL: Chenin Blanc

If we're going to talk about looking outside of the usual suspects, we have to talk about Malgas, South Africa. It's a newly formed wine region in South Africa that has exactly one, yes one, producer in it. But it's a good one. Winemaker David De Trafford was attracted to the area because its poor and rocky soil, dry climate, and ocean breezes would offer something unique. He hoped. Time will tell if others will join him in settling this area, but so far he's done great things with his big Chenin Blanc/Viognier blends. This is a region to keep an eye on.

WHAT TO EAT WITH
— 9W WINES —

Creamy and smooth, with increasing roundness and intensity,
*the 9W wines beg for you to throw something big at them. They're
unabashedly New World, and flaunt their fruit, oak, and richness.
These wines would ruin a delicate ceviche or briny oyster, but paired
with richly flavored meats, the experience is one to remember.*

BALSAMIC HONEY
PULLED PORK SLIDERS

**Recipe for
Just a Taste
Balsamic Honey
Pulled Pork**

**A mix of
green and
red cabbage,
or buy a
pre-sliced bag
of slaw (I do!)**

**2 carrots,
shredded**

**2-4 scallions,
sliced**

**½ fresh
pineapple**

1 mango, sliced

**Sliced jicama,
optional**

We love pulled pork in all its forms. Traditional barbecue-style pulled pork is easy to find in restaurants, so at home we try to mix it up. Our absolute favorite is Balsamic Honey Pulled Pork from the *Just a Taste* blog. Bathed in a sweet and salty sauce, a simple boneless pork shoulder is transformed into deeply flavored meat in just 8 hours. The richness of the meal works with the richness of the wine, but to truly make the pairing work, I top our sliders with a tropical slaw.

Make the pulled pork: Start by combining honey, balsamic vinegar, blackberry jam, hoisin sauce, chicken broth, a handful of minced garlic cloves, and half of an onion, diced; pour it over a 2- to 3-pound pork shoulder set in a slow cooker, and cook on low for 8 hours. Remove the pork and shred. Mix a tablespoon of cornstarch with 3 tablespoons of cold water, add to the slow-cooker liquid and reduce in a saucepan until thickened. Pour over the shredded pork. When it's just about ready, combine the slaw ingredients. You can make the tropical salsa vinaigrette in 1W (page 29; I add a little orange juice) or make a dressing with pineapple juice, rice vinegar, shallots, oil, salt, and pepper. Serve the pork on slider rolls and top with heaps of slaw.

PERFECT
PAIRINGS

BLT on brioche
....
Bacon turkey burgers
....
Foie gras and paté
....
Sole Meunière
....
Lobster pizza

FOODS TO
AVOID

Raw vegetable flavors

ONE TO TRY

LA GRANGE DE PIAUGIER BLANC (CÔTES DU RHÔNE, FRANCE)

AS YOU'RE SEEING THROUGHOUT THIS book, many wine regions in France were devastated by World War II, and the Rhône Valley was no exception. The region has a winemaking history that dates back to the Roman conquest under Julius Caesar, but post-war production fell off sharply in both quantity and quality. The region's revival in the late '70s and '80s gave rise to the prominence that the area enjoys today, and is a well-deserved comeback. The Rhône wines are some of the most popular and palate-friendly in the world.

Domaine de Piaugier finds its home in the village of Sablet in the Southern Rhône, an area characterized by more mild winters and hotter summers than their neighbors in the Northern Rhône. Piaugier is run by husband-and-wife team Jean-Marc and Sophie Autran, on vineyard sites that have been farmed for four generations by Jean-Marc's family. Jean-Marc grew up in the family business, and had to lure Sophie from the city to his tiny town. But love won out, and together they run the business, with Sophie working as the winemaker. Over the years, they have cobbled together

30 hectares of small vineyard sites around Sablet and are producing thoughtful, balanced wines that resist what some call the region's Achilles heel: wines made with overly ripe fruit.

Being located so close to Gigondas, an AOC that makes only red and rosé wine, it's highly unusual to dedicate vineyards to white wine production, but Jean-Marc believes that his sites, which have sandy soil, are better suited to white grape varietals. To date, they make three white wines, and the

La Grange is our favorite. Made of Grenache Blanc, Viognier, and Roussanne, this wine is a shining example of how the blended Rhône varietals truly exceed the sum of their parts. Despite being unoaked, this warm weather, ripe fruit blend has plenty of richness and body. The lack of oak aging lets its complex acidity (thanks Roussanne!) shine through, adding interesting layers to its youthful fruitiness. This wine is natural territory for Chardonnay lovers to explore. It is rare to find a French wine of this body, so enjoy this unique discovery.

LET'S PAIR IT
Fried Chicken Sammie

The Grange de Piaugier Blanc smells like a beguiling summer garden in full bloom, but this Rhône blend has a hefty, full body that can stand up to the heaviest of meals, even Gabriel's delicious **Fried Chicken Sammie.** One bite and you'll see that this pairing is like the best parts of summer rolled up in every sip and bite: pretty, floral aromas; crispy fried chicken; briny pickles; crunchy red onion. Despite being full-bodied, this wine packs some powerful acid, which cuts right through the crust of the chicken. There's no need to pack a picnic when you can recreate summer any time of year with this pairing!

FRIED CHICKEN SAMMIE

SERVES 4

This one takes a little planning—I usually start the brine the day before I make these sandwiches so that it has time to cool. But starting with the brine will ensure a deeply flavorful piece of fried bird. And get your buns from a bakery, for goodness sake. Challah, brioche, Portuguese, and potato would all be great choices here. —GABRIEL

In a small pot over medium heat, sweat the onion in oil for 2 minutes, stirring occasionally. Add the carrot and celery and cook for an additional two minutes. The vegetables should be softening, not caramelizing. Turn the heat to high, add the garlic, pepper, fennel seed, anise, rosemary, and thyme, and cook, stirring constantly, for 1 minute, until the spices and herbs are fragrant. Add the water, and once it boils, turn the heat off and stir in the salt and sugar; continue stirring until they dissolve. Remove the brine from the heat, transfer it to a bowl, and refrigerate until chilled or overnight.

CHICKEN BRINE

2 tablespoons canola oil

1 Spanish onion, sliced

1 carrot, sliced into
½-inch rounds

1 stalk celery, sliced into
½-inch rounds

2 cloves of garlic, halved

1 teaspoon
black peppercorns

1 teaspoon fennel seed

1 star anise

2 sprigs rosemary

2 sprigs thyme

2 cups water

4 tablespoons kosher salt

2 tablespoons sugar

FRIED CHICKEN SAMMIES

4 boneless chicken
thighs, skin on

2 cups flour

1 tablespoon baking powder

½ teaspoon cayenne

1 teaspoon onion powder

1 teaspoon garlic powder

1 tablespoon paprika

2 tablespoons ground
black pepper

1 teaspoon kosher salt

2 cups buttermilk

3-4 cups canola oil,
depending on the width of
your pan (enough to just
cover the chicken)

3 tablespoons mayo

2 tablespoons
honey mustard

4 buns

4 pieces of Bibb lettuce

4 thick slices of red onion

Bread and butter pickles

FRIED CHICKEN SAMMIES

Preheat oven to 250°F. Place a wire rack over a baking sheet and set aside.

Place the thighs in the cold brine and let sit for 30 minute, or up to 2 hours. Meanwhile, in a large bowl, combine the flour, baking powder, cayenne, onion powder, garlic powder, paprika, pepper, and salt, and combine with a whisk until they are well incorporated. Pour the buttermilk in a separate bowl. Remove the thighs from the brine and roll them in the dredge, tapping off any excess flour. Dip the thighs in the buttermilk, and allow excess buttermilk to drip off before placing thighs back in the dredge a second time.

Heat 3 to 4 cups of canola oil in a wide, heavy-bottomed pan until the temperature reaches 350°F. Fry the chicken thighs for 10 to 12 minutes, flipping every so often until they are deep golden in color and fully cooked through. Remove the chicken from the oil and place on the wire rack over the baking sheet. Keep the chicken warm in the oven while you assemble the sandwiches.

To assemble, combine the mayo and honey mustard and spread the mixture on the bottom slice of each bun. Top with fried chicken thigh, lettuce, onion, pickles, and top bun, and serve.

GIFTING WINE

We've all been there: You're invited over for dinner. You totally meant to spend the last year collecting unique hostess gifts for moments such as these, storing them pre-wrapped and clearly labeled in your closet, but you chose to binge watch YouTube clips of *The Daily Show* and online shoe shop instead. Pressed for time, and not wanting to arrive empty-handed, you pop into your local wine store for a nice bottle to bring. And there you stand, facing a nearly impossible task: picking wine for another person. Don't panic. Here's how to choose the right bottle.

Set Your Budget

Be firm on your price point before you walk into the store. If you can only spend $20 that's fine! Just make sure to choose a thoughtful and unique bottle.

How Many Bottles to Gift

One festively wrapped bottle is fine for a dinner party, but choose more if you're staying for the weekend. Themed gifts are always a hit: Three Pinot Noirs from around the world, for example, will make any Pinot Noir lover beam with happiness—and get you invited back.

Get Some Insider Information

I always ask our host what is planned for dinner so that we can bring a well-paired bottle. Also, if you let your host know that you are bringing wine, it ensures you'll get to partake in the bottle you brought, as opposed to seeing it whisked into the kitchen, never to be seen (or drunk) by you again.

Think Lifestyle

The more information you can give the staff at your wine store, the better. For instance, if your friend just got back from a trip to Italy (or has always wanted to travel there), bringing Italian wine feels thoughtful and personalized. Also, think about the wine knowledge of your host. If they're just getting into wine, choose a more typical varietal and region (i.e. Sauvignon Blanc from Sonoma). If you know they love trying new wine, ask for help choosing a bottle with a unique varietal or region.

Don't Be Shy

If you brought a great bottle of wine, it's okay to politely ask your host to open it. Just tell them why you're so excited for it, and why you'd like to share the experience with them. Who can resist honest enthusiasm?

Skip the Sparkling (Most of the Time)

We love sparkling wine, so it pains us to say this, but, too often, gifts of sparkling wine sit on the shelf, waiting for an "occasion" to be opened. Only gift sparkling wine when *you* are the occasion, and can make sure the bottle gets popped and enjoyed in the moment.

Know Your Audience

If your friend hates wine (gasp!) but loves whiskey, then don't bring a bottle of wine. Taking a moment to get them what they really like is more important than bringing them the tried-and-true gift.

THE
REDS

CHAPTER 5

OUR RED JOURNEY BEGINS

The staff members at The Urban Grape, as well as our customers, love white wine, and we search high and low to find the most unique bottles to sell. But despite that collective love of whites, most wine drinkers will readily admit that red wine is where concepts like winemaker influence and wine aging get really interesting. We've got a lot to talk about over the next five chapters! Once again, it all starts with cool climate, light-bodied wines. But unlike their white counterparts, these lighter, "lemonade" red wines beg for food—specifically fat and salt—in order to become truly expressive. There are red Porch Pounders, but not in this chapter!

ONE TO TRY

MARCEL LAPIERRE "RAISINS GAULOIS" GAMAY (BEAUJOLAIS, FRANCE)

ONE OF THE MOST FAMOUS AND well-known 1R regions is Beaujolais in France, long lauded for its production of the ancient, black-skinned Gamay grape. Americans reach for Beaujolais Nouveau at Thanksgiving but the region has much more to offer, and its popularity is gaining as a year-round wine. Light, fresh, and fruity, Gamay is a whole new red wine experience, often even for seasoned wine drinkers.

Like so many French winemaking regions, Beaujolais was reeling after the Second World War. Faced with a need to get their region's wine production up and running again as quickly as possible, most winemakers turned away from traditional farming and winemaking. They adopted techniques aimed at producing high yields of grapes that could make it into the market quickly. The Beaujolais Nouveau marketing campaign was born, and because of it, the region could count on an influx of cash each November. The first generation of Lapierre winemakers, Michele, adopted these post-war techniques, built a business and a life, and passed the vineyard to his son, Marcel, in 1973.

In the early 1980s, Marcel was one of the first producers in Beaujolais to embrace the idea of returning to the region's traditional winemaking. He was instrumental in the rebirth of the region's best practices through his steadfast use of organic farming and natural wine producing techniques. His influence on the region and its winemaking cannot be overstated. It is because of him that we see interesting Beaujolais wines on our shelves, as opposed to just Beaujolais Nouveau. When Marcel died at the age of 60 from cancer, he left the estate in the hands of his son and daughter, Mathieu and Camille. They ably continue the legacy of their father, and adhere to his belief that the region of Beaujolais can be known for producing joyous wines that also exhibit nuanced quality.

While most of the Lapierre wines are structured and meant to be taken seriously, their "Raisins Gaulois" is decidedly fun and very quaffable. Drink this wine all year long with a slight chill and a savory dinner. It's a favorite of our staff, and of all who are lucky enough to find themselves with a glass.

LET'S PAIR IT
Potato and Rosemary Pizza

Wine and food pairings don't always need to be complex; in fact, sometimes the more effortless the components, the better they complement one another. **With a relaxed and rustic wine like the "Raisins Gaulois" all you really need to complete the experience is a relaxed and rustic meal like a Potato and Rosemary Pizza.** The creaminess of the potatoes and saltiness of each bite of pizza softens the vibrant acidity of the wine, while the rosemary brings out the Gamay's natural earthiness. This pairing is so addictive that you'll want to make several pizzas and have a second bottle (and some willing friends) ready to go!

POTATO AND ROSEMARY PIZZA

SERVES 2 TO 4

4 cups warm water

1 tablespoon kosher salt

2 pounds Yukon gold potatoes, peeled

5 tablespoons extra virgin olive oil

Cracked black pepper

1 ball of prepared pizza dough

4 sprigs rosemary leaves

We are going to start by assuming that this isn't the first pizza you've made. So, do the pizza thing that you do: buy a dough, make a dough, use a stone or a steel, fire up your beehive or your green egg, preheat your oven, or crank up your broiler. If you want to learn how to make your own dough, look up Jim Leahy's excellent recipe. —GABRIEL

Preheat grill to high heat or an oven to 500°F.

In a medium bowl, stir together the warm water and the salt until dissolved. Using a mandolin or very sharp knife, thinly slice the potatoes (like potato chip-thin) and add them to the water. Let them soak for 10 minutes or up to 1 hour. Drain the water and add 4 tablespoons of olive oil and a little cracked black pepper to the potatoes and toss to combine. Roll out the pizza dough to your desired size. Lay the potatoes on top of the dough, either in a fish scale pattern or randomly. Top with the rosemary and the remaining olive oil. Grill or bake the pizza until the dough is cooked through and the edges are just starting to brown.

HAVE WINE, WILL PICNIC

THE FUN OF LEARNING ABOUT RED wine is that things ramp up much more quickly than they do for white wines. There are a lot of moving pieces, and they happen earlier on the Progressive Scale.

So, even though we're still in the world of very light-bodied wines with lots of bright, lip-smacking acid, we're already starting to see winemaker influences on the wine that change the end product. Pinot Noir, one of

climate	Cool climates with some maritime and alpine influence
regions	Central Otago, New Zealand; Sonoma Coast, California; Burgundy and Loire Valley, France; Willamette Valley, Oregon; Piedmont, Italy
varietals	Pinot Noir, Gamay, Barbera, Dolcetto
technique	Short maceration; primarily steel or cement egg fermentation with limited oak aging
characteristics	Light-bodied and lean with a mouthfeel resembling skim milk; tart and acidic.
color	Transparent, ruby red with some purple highlights
ideal pairings	Tomatoes; savory herbs; mushrooms; red fruits; salmon; beef carpaccio; Thanksgiving flavors

the world's most important varietals, still dominates this part of the Progressive Scale.

For the most part, the wine-growing regions that produce 2R wines are still temperamental. Colder shoulder seasons may or may not blossom into ideal growing seasons. A perfect example of this is Burgundy, which has had a multi-year stretch of vintages impacted by late frost and damaging hail storms. But once the growing season gets going, there is warming sun and a good stretch of temperate weather.

Winemakers are also starting to assert their gentle influence over the finished product. It may be as simple as moving harvest earlier or later, in order to adjust acidity or ripeness. Considerations like extended maceration, length of fermentation, and oak treatment also come into play much earlier for red wines. In general, red wines need a second fermentation process called malolactic fermentation, or ML (see page 67), in order to be palatable; therefore, winemakers also have to plan for, and monitor, this important technique. All of these influences have to be kept in balance with the grapes, so the wine's natural light-bodied tendencies can shine through. Winemaking is always a balancing act, but this low on the red wine scale, it's a tightrope act.

Despite the first inklings of juiciness and creaminess, what separates 2R wines from the next step up on the scale is their

need for food. Just like 1R, their high acid demands food with fat and salt to really bring out their true beauty. That's why, to us, 2R wines are the ultimate picnic wines. Pack a meal of charcuterie, paté, and salty hard cheeses for a sublime experience.

GEEKOUT:
UNDERSTANDING WINE CLONES

At UG, we often like to taste wines made with the same grape and by the same producer, but that have been grown in different microclimates. It helps us understand the part that terroir plays on a wine. But it's not *all* about terroir; as it turns out, grape varietal clones are an important part of the conversation, and one that people really don't talk about. Why? Because, it's confusing.

No grape has more clones than Pinot Noir. The popular grape is considered genetically unstable, and mutates easily into new versions of itself. These versions diverge over time, and become known for different qualities: early bud break, mildew resistance, higher quality fruit, intense floral aromas, denser color—the list goes on and on. Winemakers grow different clonal varieties depending on their terroir, or their winemaking goals.

The best winemakers blend different Pinot Noir clones together to produce a wine that incorporates nuances that they could not get with one clone alone. The average wine drinker does not need to worry about clonal variety at all because good winemakers will work the clones on your behalf. But it sure is fun to know that all Pinot Noir grapes are not the same. In fact, they're changing with every generation.

Our Favorite Regions and Varietals

Specific areas of the wine-growing world simply have a lockdown on the lightest-bodied red wines, so although we've started to see some changes, we haven't really moved too far geographically. These micro-changes in terroir or in the composition of the grape varietal demonstrate how sensitive the final wine is to the elements that influence the grape itself.

FRANCE

REGION: Burgundy
VARIETAL: Pinot Noir

The French system of ever-narrowing spheres of designation around their appellations, regions, sub-regions, and communes can be confusing. It's helpful to use the imagery of Google Earth to understand how they designate wine areas. For this example, 2R starts zoomed out on the region of Burgundy and then zooms in to the appellation of Côte d'Or, which becomes further specified as a sub-appellation of Côte de Nuit, and the commune of Morey-St. Denis. Each commune is distinguished because of its specific terroir and microclimate. Morey-St. Denis is known for producing more masculine Pinot Noirs than neighboring communes in Burgundy. These slightly richer and fuller-bodied wines are excellent food wines, and often less expensive than wines from more well-known zip codes, such as Gevrey-Chambertin.

ITALY

REGION: Piedmont
VARIETAL: Barbera

Piedmont, a region located in the Northwest corner of Italy, is best known for wines made from the Nebbiolo grape—but it has other incredible offerings, too. We're showing our bias here, but the wines of Piedmont dominate our lighter-bodied red wines at the store. Barbera is one of our favorites. Barbera was historically a simple, regional table wine, meant to be paired with everyday fare. Regionally and internationally, no one took it as seriously as Nebbiolo. But in a world where simple tastes and pleasures are making a comeback, Barbera's popularity has steadily grown. Barbera's highly toned acidity and subtle structure go perfectly with charcuterie and cheese, or a pasta with fresh tomato sauce. We're fans of Dolcetto, too, another Piedmont wine with similar body.

NEW ZEALAND

REGION: Central Otago
VARIETAL: Pinot Noir

Far away places sometimes get grouped together, and we know that for a lot of people it's easy to lump the wines of New Zealand and Australia together. But in terms of climate and wine growing, they're very different beasts. New Zealand's red wine offerings are influenced by a huge diurnal shift and colder shoulder seasons, while we won't see grapes grown in Australia's warmer climate until much later on the Progressive Scale. The Pinot Noirs made in Central Otago, one of New Zealand's most successful regions, are lush and intense. Made with little winemaker intervention, they showcase the area's unique terroir and microclimates.

WHAT TO EAT WITH
— 2R WINES —

The wines that we categorize into 2R come from some of the most *influential regions in the world, and sometimes the tendency is to feel that these wines have to stand on ceremony with a fancy dinner. We say, "No way." At their core, the wines are rustic and simple, and often pair best with food that is the same. The only requirement we see is to pair them with a meal that adds a little salt and fat, to help them relax into their full expression.*

GRILLED CHEESE AND TOMATO SOUP

This is the meal that makes kids of all ages deliriously happy. It doesn't matter if your soup comes from a can, a Tetra Pak, or is made from scratch. For this pairing to work, it just needs to be super tomato-y, so that it brings out the natural tomato plant aromas and flavors of 2R wines. The fat and the salt in the cheese are kept from overwhelming the wine thanks to the brightly acidic, tomato explosion from both the soup and pairing.

We have a lot of favorite tomato soup recipes but as a family we prefer versions that have passed through an immersion or traditional blender. And because we're pairing to wine that is light-bodied, we recommend skipping the cream. To feed a crowd (and even a small family is a crowd when grilled cheese is involved), I grab a big loaf of sourdough bread and hunt for every scrap of cheese in our fridge. Uniformity in flavor is frowned upon, and one of the best parts of the meal is not knowing exactly what cheese is hidden in your sandwich. Then we fire up the griddle, grill the sammies in butter, and bring the towering stack and the pot of soup to the table for family-style service. It's a perfect end to any day.

PERFECT PAIRINGS

Salmon

Beef carpaccio

Tomatoes

Savory herbs

Mushrooms

Red fruits

Thanksgiving flavors

FOODS TO AVOID

Cream sauces

ONE TO TRY

MOUTON NOIR "OTHER PEOPLE'S PINOT" PINOT NOIR (WILLAMETTE VALLEY, OREGON)

WE COULDN'T WRITE A WINE EDUCATION book without including the person in the industry with which we feel the most kismet connection, André Hueston Mack of Mouton Noir. From the stories of his early days, when he worked at McDonald's, to his love of ridiculously funny puns, to his guiding belief that wine is, after all, just grape juice, André and TJ share a lot of resumé highlights. The night the two of them ran a Geek Out class together at The Urban Grape stands out as a highlight on our wine journey.

André didn't start out in the wine business, but not many people do unless you've had a winery handed down to you by the previous generation. A creative and energetic person, he left a desk job after catching the wine bug, and worked his way up in restaurants until he was the head sommelier at Thomas Keller's Per Se in New York. In 2007, he worked his wine industry contacts in Oregon to start his own label, Mouton Noir, a nickname that stuck from his days as the "black sheep" of New York's fine dining wine culture.

As the costs of prime acreage, winemaking facilities, and wine production skyrocket, André represents a growing number of "garage" winemakers, people with no land of their own who buy grapes and rent facility space to produce excellent wines that are approachable and affordable. This generation of winemakers isn't giving the finger to the storied history of winemaking as much as they are elbowing their way into the game and demanding to be part of the story. André's fun labels, affordable price points, accessible life story, and speaking

tours (check out his TEDx talk), make newer wine drinkers feel like they can elbow in on this world, too. After all, as he says, it's just grape juice.

It's fitting, too, that André sources his grapes from Oregon, a state once considered the black sheep of the American winemaking scene. With a climate strikingly similar to Burgundy and a dedication to Pinot Noir, Oregon's wines are now considered some of the best in the world, and are growing in popularity with every passing year. "OPP" knocks it out of the park on all levels: It's affordable, it's a solid representation of Oregon Pinot Noir, and it's just irreverent enough to take intimidation out of the whole experience. Here's to people like André and TJ, who are inspiring a new generation of black sheep to join them in the wine world.

LET'S PAIR IT
Slow-Roasted Salmon over Bacon-Braised Cabbage

Pinot Noir is an exceptional food wine, and it has some classic pairings—beef bourguignon and salmon being two of our favorites. **That's why we knew we had to pair Gabriel's Slow Roasted Salmon and Bacon-Braised Cabbage with Mouton Noir O.P.P Pinot Noir from Oregon.** Both elements share a common origin on the Northwest coast, which always makes for a good pairing. In addition, the fattiness of the fish and saltiness of the bacon turn the O.P.P., which is already an outstanding wine, into something even more vibrant. The interplay between food and wine is apparent in every bite, with the wine's bright, fresh, red fruit flavor shining through. This push-pull between the various components is the sign of a perfect pairing.

SLOW-ROASTED SALMON
over **BACON-BRAISED CABBAGE**

SERVES 4

Wild fish is ideal here because farm-raised fish lacks both the fattiness and flavor that are emphasized in this preparation. Just make sure that the fish pieces are of similar thickness. You'll see that I ask you to cover the baking dish with plastic wrap—this is not a joke. The salmon will not change color very much as it cooks, and will remain amazingly moist.   —GABRIEL

SLOW-ROASTED SALMON

Four 6-ounce pieces of salmon

Kosher salt and cracked black pepper

1 tablespoon ground coriander

1 tablespoon picked thyme leaves

1 shallot, minced

1 tablespoon butter, melted

1 tablespoon extra virgin olive oil

Juice of one lemon

Preheat oven to 210°F.

Season the salmon with salt and pepper. In a small bowl, combine the cracked coriander, thyme, shallot, butter, and olive oil. Spread the mixture evenly over the pieces of salmon. Place the salmon in a buttered, oven-safe dish. Cover the dish tightly with plastic wrap and then place it in the oven. Cook for approximately 25 minutes, or until a fork inserted in the middle comes out warm. Drizzle lemon juice over top of each fillet. Take care when removing the salmon from the dish as it will be very fragile. Serve over Bacon-Braised Cabbage with Apple Rosemary Puree.

BACON-BRAISED CABBAGE

6 ounces slab bacon, cut into ½-inch *batons*

1 large onion, diced

1 large carrot, peeled, quartered, and cut into ¼-inch thick pieces

4 cloves garlic, sliced

1 head green cabbage, cored and sliced

Kosher salt and cracked black pepper

1 tablespoon red wine vinegar

2 tablespoons parsley leaves, sliced

BACON-BRAISED CABBAGE

In a medium saucepot, cook bacon in batches over medium-high heat until crispy. Transfer bacon to a paper towel-lined plate and reserve the fat in the pot. Turn the heat to medium-low and add the onion. Cook until the onion becomes translucent, 2 to 3 minutes. Add the carrots and cook for 2 minutes, then add the garlic, and cook for an additional 2 minutes. Add the cabbage. Season with salt and pepper. Stir for 1 to 2 minutes, until the cabbage has been lightly coated in the fat. Cover and turn the heat down to low and cook for 20 to 30 minutes, stirring occasionally, until the cabbage is mostly tender with just a little bite. Check the seasoning, add the vinegar and reserved bacon, and when ready to serve, fold in the parsley.

APPLE ROSEMARY PUREE

2½ tablespoons unsalted butter

1 sprig rosemary

5 ounces white wine

1½ tablespoons sugar

3 Golden Delicious or Fuji apples

1 clove

1 star anise

1 cinnamon stick

Sachet or empty tea bag

APPLE ROSEMARY PUREE

In a small pot, brown the butter over medium-low heat until it bubbles and starts to smell very nutty. Remove it from the heat and add the sprig of rosemary. Let stand. In a medium bowl, combine the white wine and sugar. Peel and slice the apples as finely as possible. Immediately place the slices in the wine solution and stir to coat. Place the clove, star anise, and cinnamon stick in the sachet or tea bag. Heat a large pan over medium-high heat, and then add the apple-wine mixture and the sachet, stirring constantly. Cook the apples until the pan is almost dry, but without letting the apples caramelize. Once cooked, remove the sachet and put the apples in a blender. Strain the butter through a coffee filter and add it to the blender, as well. Puree until smooth, and then pass it through a fine strainer. Serve immediately or refrigerate and reheat when ready to serve.

WINE WITH BUBBLES

Bubbly wine is a book unto itself, and an often-misunderstood segment that includes Cava, Prosecco, Cremant, Champagne, Franciacorta, and Lambrusco, to name but a few. Despite the fact that it's considered by many to be a special occasion or cocktail hour drink, sparkling wine actually tastes best when it is paired with food. Many older, vintage Champagnes are able to stand up to the richest of dishes.

There are many ways to make sparkling wine (including just pumping bubbles into still wine, a.k.a. the CO_2 method), but these are our three preferred methods.

Méthode Traditionelle

The word "Champagne" has incorrectly come to mean all dry wine with bubbles, but it actually refers just to sparkling wines made in the tiny region of Champagne, France. While these are undoubtedly some of the best sparkling wines in the world, they are traditionally the most expensive. If you love Champagne and want to try other similar options, look for wines made in the Traditional Method, or Méthode Traditionelle. These wines have gone through a secondary fermentation inside the bottle, which creates CO_2 and adds naturally occurring carbonation. The wines are then aged in the bottle, laying on their sides to collect the dead yeast cells, which are eventually disgorged. A small amount of liqueur, called dosage, is usually added to the bottles, which are then re-corked and sent to market. Even if they are not from Champagne, traditional method sparkling wines often have a body and taste that are similar to Champagne.

Charmat Method

Another popular method for making sparkling wine is the Charmat method, which is used for Prosecco. These wines undergo secondary fermentation inside a large tank before they are bottled, and generally have a fresher taste and lighter body because they have not

TRADITIONAL METHOD SPARKLING WINE

DRIEST

BN	BRUT NATURE
BX	EXTRA BRUT
B	BRUT
DX	EXTRA DRY
D	DRY
S	SEC
DS	DEMI-SEC
X	DOUX

SWEETEST

Popular Examples

CHAMPAGNE (FRANCE)

CREMANT (FRANCE)

CAVA (SPAIN)

FRANCIACORTA (ITALY)

been aged in bottle. This method costs the winemaker less money, which is why sparkling wines made in this way are usually less expensive.

Ancestral Method

In the "everything old is new again" category, Ancestral Method, or "Pet Nat," wines are bursting on to the scene, much to everyone's delight. These funky sparklers are bottled during their primary fermentation, catching the first round of bubbles that occur when the yeast eats the sugar in the grape. Often sealed with a crown cap (like a beer bottle) and tasting a little funky and natural, these wines are very different, but worth seeking out.

Designations of Sweetness

Wines made in the Méthode Traditionelle, including Champagne, Cava, Cremant, and other popular sparkling wines, use a confusing system to designate the level of the wine's sweetness. The system moves from Brut Nature (driest) to Doux (sweetest). If you have as much trouble remembering that as we do, this infographic should help make sense of it all. We prefer to pair Extra Brut and Brut with our meals; Demi-Sec makes a wonderful pairing for dessert.

Prosecco has fewer stops on its designation system, moving from Brut (driest) to Demi-Sec (sweetest).

CHAPTER 6

ENTICINGLY DELICIOUS

A lot of new wine drinkers lean towards sweet red wines because they are intimidated by red wine's tannic structure and dry finish. When these sweet wine drinkers come into The Urban Grape, we try to direct them into the forgiving landscape of 3R and 4R wines. Undeniably juicy, with low tannin and structure, these wines are all made in a dry style, but their enticing fruitiness helps to lure new drinkers into the beguiling world of red wine. Even experienced red wine drinkers can't resist the siren call of these palate-friendly wines. So, pour a glass and start sipping. Also note: Food will enhance the experience, but is not required.

3R

THE YUMMY FACTOR

OF ALL THE DESCRIPTORS USED throughout wine history, there is one that we think is chronically *under*used: YUMMY. At The Urban Grape, we use it a lot for wines all over the Progressive Scale, but no group has more of a yumminess factor than 3R (and its big brother, 7R).

One of the things that makes wine yummy: unabashed fruitiness. If TJ comes in to the kitchen at dinnertime and asks what wine I'm in the mood for, he knows if I say "a yummy one" that he needs to go on the hunt for something with low tannins, lots of fruit, and an approachable juiciness. It sounds like I'm

AT A GLANCE

climate	Temperate warmth, but some regions see more sun than others
regions	Burgundy, France; Willamette Valley, Oregon; Anderson Valley and Russian River Valley, California; Etna and Piedmont, Italy; Long Island, New York
varietals	Pinot Noir, Nerello Mascalese, Barbera, Cabernet Franc
technique	A variety of techniques; cooler regions use mix of longer maceration, some barrel fermentation and aging; warmer climates use cement or stainless-steel aging and less oak
characteristics	Light- to medium-bodied with a mouthfeel resembling 1% milk; juicy with ripe fruit and vibrant acidity
color	Semi-transparent; ruby red to brick in color
ideal pairings	Grilled seafood; capers and olives; tomatoes and tomato sauces; pizza; salmon and tuna; salty/fatty appetizers; earthy vegetables

asking for something sweet, but all of these wines have fruit without sweetness, and a dry finish. Most importantly, they have "pop and pour" ability, and taste just as good without food as they do paired with dinner.

The naturally low-tannin, thinnest-skinned grapes that we saw in 1R and 2R are still here in 3R, but they are being grown in warmer climates with more sun. They're also growing in more forgiving soil, which means more water makes it into the grape, plumping it up and creating a fuller-bodied drinking experience. Wines like Pinot Noir that were thinner and more astringent in 2R, find lushness with all this easy living. Winemakers are also utilizing oak treatment somewhere in the winemaking process, which imparts even more softness. All this adds up to easy-drinking, fruit-forward yum.

While regions like Burgundy and grapes like Dolcetto are still present, their influence is waning, and new regions and thicker-skinned grapes are making their first appearance. Tempranillo, Nebbiolo, Sangiovese, Nerllo Mascalese, Cabernet Franc—what a list of grapes to start exploring! These grapes are coming from cooler climates and aren't seeing much oak finishing yet, so we're getting them in their raw form. Left on their own, these grapes are vibrant, bright, juicy, and fun—and not yet the more serious, medium- and full-bodied wines that they will become.

3R is like the *Yo Gabba Gabba!* of the wine world: worth exploring, filled with happy and carefree characters, and theme songs that go like: "There's a party in my tummy, so yummy, so yummy!"

GEEKOUT:
KNOW YOUR FARMER

Lots of people will scour a farmers' market for the perfect organic tomato, but then pick up a bottle of mass-produced grocery store wine on the way home. Like a perfect meal, wine is made or broken by its ingredients, and those ingredients are grown on farms. If you live a farm-to-table lifestyle, you should consider living a farm-to-glass lifestyle, too, and know where your wine comes from. Here's how to do that.

In general, try not to buy wines that are backed by big advertising campaigns. Big producers need big yields, which means less quality control, more synthetic chemicals, and less nuanced wine. If you're buying an $8 wine that you heard of through a multi-million-dollar ad buy, you should know that you're drinking about 10 cents worth of wine (if that). Instead of buying something cheap and mass-produced from the most famous regions, look for higher quality, less expensive wine made by family-owned vineyards in up-and-coming regions. For roughly the same price, you'll have a much better wine experience.

Lastly, even some of the best winemakers source fruit—but there should be transparency. Be wary of producers and wine clubs that won't tell you where their fruit comes from. Reputable winemakers want you to know point of origin, because that's part of the wine's terroir and story. Most importantly, build a relationship with a trusted wine shop. They'll always help you find the best quality wines for your budget.

Our Favorite Regions and Varietals

Things are beefing up all over the world. Each region seems to have its own offering for fruity, lighter-bodied, low tannin red wine, most likely because it is an important counterpart to the more serious, fuller-bodied red wines that pair with the main course of a meal. You'll notice a trend binding these regions together: a strong maritime influence on the growing season and grapes.

UNITED STATES

REGION: Willamette Valley, Oregon
VARIETAL: Pinot Noir

Burgundy's dominance over Pinot Noir has ended, and now other regions can have their moment to shine. Whatever you do, don't mispronounce the winemaking region of Willamette to a person from Oregon or you'll be rebuked with "It's Will-am-it, dammit!" The Yamhill-Carlton AVA produces some of our favorite Pinot Noirs from the north of this region. It didn't become a winemaking AVA until 2004, but farming itself is not new to this area, thanks to layers of marine fossils and fertile lands fed naturally by the Yamhill River. Although richer in style than French Pinot Noir, the wine being made here is so balanced that even Burgundian winemakers have taken notice and given their respect. (Some have even opened up shop here.)

UNITED STATES

REGION: Sonoma Coast, California
VARIETAL: Pinot Noir

Sonoma Coast Pinot Noir is strikingly different from its Burgundian counterpart, but it's no less renowned. Despite being influenced by the cool, California coastal winds, the region receives more sunshine per day, and per growing season, than does Burgundy. These West Coast grapes are naturally plumper and less acidic than their French counterparts, leading to softer wines. Sonoma also has different soils than Burgundy, so the mineral essence of the wine is different, too. Fanatics will argue about which region makes the best expression of Pinot Noir. But why argue when both regions have so much incredible wine to offer?

UNITED STATES

REGION: Long Island, New York
VARIETAL: Cabernet Franc

When it comes to American wine regions, the East Coast plays a distant second fiddle to California, Oregon, and Washington. Long Island is the little region that could, producing more interesting and well-regarded wines with each vintage. Red wine varietals like Merlot, Malbec, and Petit Verdot are growing well in the region, although are often lighter in body and tannin than their counterparts grown in other, better known regions. We prefer the area's light-bodied Cabernet Franc wines that pair fruit flavors and gentle spice with the grape's signature green vegetal-ness. Cabernet Franc from the Finger Lakes region of New York is also spectacular.

WHAT TO EAT WITH
— 3R WINES —

Fruity and fabulous, these wines have low tannins, lots of fruit,
*and bring an ease and joy to your glass. Because the grapes for
these wines are grown in warmer climates than the wines in 1R
and 2R, they're rounder and softer and drink well with or without
food. This makes them perfect cocktail party wines. We're not seeing
too much oak aging yet, so the wines still exhibit unadulterated
brightness in both acidity and fruit.*

PIZZA NIGHT!

There was a time in our lives, when The Urban Grape was just getting going and the kids were little, when the local pizza place was on heavy, heavy rotation. We still love our pizza nights, but now have fun firing up the oven and making a wide variety of pies at home. 3R wines go so well with make-your-own-pizza nights because you can tailor every pie to be a sensational pairing.

First and foremost, I never make my own dough, so let's not even pretend. And sometimes we just use bagels or naan, so let's *really* not pretend. In small bowls, lay out a wide variety of ingredients. Our favorites include: leftover homemade sauce (see page 175); a few different cheeses, like mozzarella and ricotta; briny additions like olives; earthy veggies like sautéed onions and mushrooms; arugula for spice; and cooked, crumbled sausage. Everyone gets half a ball of dough to roll out and shape, and finish with his or her unique combination of toppings. Whether it's a plain cheese or an everything pizza, it's going to pair perfectly with your wine.

Remember: These 3R wines are also great cocktail party wines, so don't be afraid to invite a crowd and serve the pizzas as appetizers right there in the kitchen.

PERFECT
PAIRINGS

Salty/fatty appetizers

Salmon and tuna

Grilled seafood

Capers and olives

Tomatoes and tomato sauces

Earthy vegetables

FOODS TO
AVOID

Rich, heavy meat dishes

ESCAROLE, MUSHROOM, AND POACHED EGG SALAD

SERVES 4

1 pound mixed mushrooms, cut into pieces of similar thickness

9 tablespoons extra virgin olive oil, divided

1 teaspoon thyme leaves

Kosher salt and cracked black pepper

2 tablespoons butter

1 head fennel, cored and cut into 1½-inch wedges

2 leeks, cut in half lengthwise

1 Honeycrisp apple

½ head of escarole, outer leaves discarded, washed

2 tablespoons parsley leaves

4 eggs

3 tablespoons white wine vinegar

1 tablespoon fresh lemon juice

¼ cup toasted hazelnuts, barely chopped

2 tablespoons shaved Parmesan

This dish is dedicated to my children, Marin and Henry, who are under the false impression that they "hate mushrooms," which leaves me no choice but to serve them fungi constantly, because I am a "bad person," and I "can't stop myself." That said, this salad benefits from a mix of mushrooms, such as oysters, buttons, chanterelles, and hen of the woods—just be sure to remove any tough, woody ones . . . and be sure to make your own kids try it. —GABRIEL

Light a grill to high heat. Preheat an oven to 450°F and place a baking sheet on the center rack.

In a medium bowl, toss the mushrooms with 5 tablespoons olive oil, thyme, salt, and pepper. Once the oven reaches 450°F, remove the baking sheet. Place the butter on the hot baking sheet and let it melt. Add the mushrooms and toss gently. Return the pan to the oven and cook for 30 minutes or until the mushrooms are golden brown and crispy.

In a medium bowl, toss the fennel pieces and leeks in 2 tablespoons olive oil, and season with salt and pepper. Grill them over the hottest part of the grill so that they get charred, but remain slightly crunchy, about 1 minute per side. Once grilled, roughly chop the leeks into ¼-inch long pieces.

Cut the apple into thin slices, and then add them to a salad bowl, along with the mushrooms, fennel, leeks, escarole, and parsley. Fill a small pot with 2 inches of salted water and bring to a boil. Turn the water down to a simmer and add the white wine vinegar. Crack the eggs into the water one at a time, using a spoon to swirl the water around the egg after each one. Let cook for about 4 minutes, or until the yolks have reached your desired runniness. While the eggs are cooking, dress the salad with the remaining 2 tablespoons olive oil and lemon juice, and season it with salt and pepper. Add the hazelnuts and Parmesan and divide the salad amongst four plates. Remove each egg from the water with a slotted spoon and place atop each salad.

4R

THE GLOBAL PASSPORT

GET READY TO EXPLORE THE FURTHEST winemaking corners of the earth, because almost every winemaking country in the world has a player in 4R. If you love to explore varietals, regions, and winemaking styles, then you will naturally gravitate toward this globally influenced grouping of progressively scaled wines.

4R is the absolute last stand for Pinot Noir, and you'll only find the bigger, American-style Pinots here. They're grown in lots of

climate	A mix of cool and temperate climates, some with maritime and alpine influences
regions	Sicily and Piedmont, Italy; Carneros and Russian River Valley, California; Bordeaux, Loire Valley, and Rhône Valley, France
varietals	Nerello Mascalese, Nerello Cappuccio, Nebbiolo, Cabernet Franc, Sangiovese, and Grenache
technique	A mix of steel and oak aging, and varying lengths of maceration
characteristics	Mouthfeel resembling 2% milk; ripe fruit, balanced acid, and subtle tannins
color	Semi-opaque red with purple and garnet tones
ideal pairings	Cured meats and sausages; grilled vegetables; steak salads; chicken dishes

sun, finished with extended oak aging, have more alcohol, and juicy fruit flavors. These wines are another example of the ways in which, thanks to full sun and a freer attitude toward experimentation, some American wines diverge from their traditional Old World roots.

Beyond Pinot Noir, grape varietals like Cabernet Franc, Grenache, Nebbiolo, and Nero D'Avola appear. These varietals, especially popular ones like Cabernet Franc and Grenache, are grown in many winemaking regions across the world. Despite different terroirs, climates, and winemaking traditions, many wines find a home in this welcoming section. The only requirements are the continuation of the juiciness found in 3R, with just a little more body, and often the start of the tannic structure that soon plays a role in red wines.

Experimentation in wine is so incredibly important, because it allows you to try new flavors and aromatics while still staying in the comfort zone of a certain mouthfeel and body of the wine. Side-by-side comparisons of wines from around the globe allow you to understand the influence of terroir in a way that is not apparent through reading alone. You'll learn more about terroir and winemaking techniques by exploring 4R than you will in almost any other section of this book. At the same time, these wines maintain enough of the yumminess factor to

be approachable for most palates. If you've got wanderlust in your heart and a wine passport that begs for stamps, you'll enjoy exploring the many zip codes and varietals contained in this section.

GEEKOUT:
INTERNATIONAL STYLE WINE

It's a wine sleight of hand that when we speak of global wines, we are *not* talking about International Style wines. How did it come to be that "global" and "international" could mean such different things?

International Style wine is code for a decades-old trend toward making wines that appeal to a specific palate, namely the American palate. In general, these wines have very ripe fruit, higher alcohol, cleaner flavors, and less nuance. Their high polish leads many to say that they lack personality (a.k.a. terroir), and yet these wines rack up the big wine review scores that matter to many buyers. International Style wines frustrate wine traditionalists, who see the trend toward sameness as ruining the distinctiveness that makes wine so endlessly intriguing.

While the pendulum once swung very far over to the International Style, we now see it swinging back into moderation. Mass-produced wines will always be formulaic, but smaller producers are taking the best of this trend—approachability and palate-friendliness—and layering it with more traditional characteristics like a sense of place and history. The resulting wines are both exciting and drinkable—a trend we think all wine drinkers can rally behind. At The Urban Grape, we encourage abundant global drinking, with a dash of International Style.

Our Favorite Regions and Varietals

Narrowing down what regions and varietals to concentrate on for 4R might have been the hardest part of writing this entire book. But when we look at our wine wall, it's Italy's indigenous varietals that crush this section. These might be our favorites, but with Pinot Noir sputtering out and other varietals filling the void, there's lots of room for exploration.

ITALY

REGION: Sicily
VARIETALS: Nerello Mascalese, Nerello Cappuccio

There is no wine region on earth quite like the Etna DOC in Sicily, Italy. If upon hearing "Etna" you immediately think "Mount Etna," you're correct. The grapes that make these intriguing wines are grown in soils laden with volcanic ash from the still active volcano. Inhospitable soil, steeply angled vineyards that rise 3,500 feet above sea level, gnarled old vines, harvests that are threatened by snow: What sounds like a farmer's nightmare is actually a winegrower's paradise. The small, hearty, red grapes that are grown in Etna, Nerello Mascalese and Nerello Cappuccio, produce wines with so much rustic elegance that the end product defies the growing conditions. The wines of Etna have caught on in the U.S., and are worth seeking out.

ITALY

REGION: Piedmont
VARIETAL: Nebbiolo

Here it is, in earnest: TJ's favorite grape, Nebbiolo. This grape is grown in regions throughout Piedmont, including the Langhe and Gattinara, as well as in the Valtellina region in Lombardy. For now, let's focus on the lighter bodied Nebbiolo wines, which you can drink without having to age for ten years first.

Nebbiolo can be tough to grow, and the lowest elevation vineyards and most northern vineyard sites tend to produce lean grapes that have only just ripened. These wines, just starting in 3R but found more in 4R, have the grape's signature rose, strawberry, and tar flavors, but with a leaner body and lots of bright acid. They're excellent food wines, made for snacking and sipping, and are generally much less expensive than their beefier, more famous peers.

FRANCE

REGION: Loire Valley
VARIETAL: Cabernet Franc

Anjou and Chinon, two regions in the middle of France's Loire Valley, are the perfect areas to exemplify the hospitable and fruit-driven 4R section. While other areas of the Loire focus on specific varietals, Anjou takes a more relaxed approach, ably growing Cabernet Franc, Cabernet Sauvignon, and Gamay, along with some lesser-known red varietals. Anjou is perhaps best known for its Cabernet Franc wines. The father of Cabernet Sauvignon, Cabernet Franc had been relegated to a supporting role as a blending wine in recent decades. But it's making a comeback as a primary varietal. The Anjou Cabernet Franc wines highlight its best characteristics: a spicy, green pepper vegetal base with ripe fruit and food-friendly acidity.

WHAT TO EAT WITH
— 4R WINES —

Globally influenced, universally adored, and just plain tasty, the 4R wines make nearly everyone happy and pair with a wide variety of foods. They love brine, starch, and cured meats, which sounds like a pretty perfect combination of food groups to us. These are also fantastic cocktail party wines, especially if you're serving cheese, charcuterie, and antipasto platters. Just make sure that your cheeses aren't too heavy and stinky, as these wines can still be overpowered.

TJ'S FAVORITE PASTA

Tomatoes (cherry, grape, small roma, or a mixture)

Olive oil

Garlic, minced

Dried oregano or basil

Salt and pepper

A mix of sweet and hot Italian sausage

1 pound orecchiette pasta

Basil pesto (we swear by *The Silver Palate's* recipe)

Parmesan cheese

We drink a lot of 4R wines in the summer because they're interesting enough to keep us thinking, but universal enough to pair with most of what we're cooking, outside of the lightest fish and salad dishes. My mom created this recipe when an abundance of August herbs and tomatoes collided with a mostly empty pantry and refrigerator. It was instantly a favorite of TJ's, and because it's basically an antipasto platter pasta, you know it pairs perfectly with the 4Rs.

Preheat oven to 250°F. Slice tomatoes in half, and rub with olive oil. Place them cut-side up on a rimmed baking sheet. Sprinkle the tomatoes with your desired amount of garlic, herbs, and salt and pepper. (We use a lot, so go for it.) Roast the tomatoes until they're softened, slightly dehydrated, and beginning to caramelize on top—the time will depend on the size. (Store leftover tomatoes in olive oil in the fridge, and serve with cheese and crackers for an easy appetizer.)

Grill sausage until browned and starting to crisp, then slice into rounds. Meanwhile, cook pasta according to directions, reserving some of the pasta water before draining. In a large bowl, combine the pasta, sausage, oven-dried tomatoes, and pesto and stir to combine. Add reserved pasta water as needed to emulsify and spread the sauce. Top with freshly grated Parmesan and serve family style.

PERFECT
PAIRINGS

Chicken dishes

Steak salads

Cured meats and sausages

Grilled vegetables

Capers and olives

FOODS TO
AVOID

Flaky white fish and other delicate seafood and shellfish

ONE TO TRY

COULY-DUTHEIL "LA COULÉE AUTOMNALE" CABERNET FRANC (LOIRE VALLEY, FRANCE)

CABERNET FRANC IS GROWN ALL OVER the world, and shows up as a medium-bodied wine on our Progressive Scale. Given its importance—it's not only the father of Cabernet Sauvignon, but is famous as a blending grape in Bordeaux and as a stand-alone varietal in regions like the Loire—we wanted to focus on it as soon as it entered the scene. No region makes lighter bodied, single-varietal Cabernet Franc wines quite like Chinon in the Loire, and no producer is more famous for expressing the varietal's characteristics than Couly-Dutheil.

Couly-Dutheil was born from two friendly and intertwined families that made things official with a well-timed marriage of cousins, Baptiste Dutheil and Marie Couly, and a second marriage of cousin René Couly to their daughter, Madeleine. Baptiste and

René worked together to build Couly-Dutheil, and their descendants have been managing the property and making exceptional wine ever since. Today, Couly-Dutheil is the largest producer in Chinon, and the family also assists other Chinon producers to distribute their wines out of the region.

As can happen with family dynasties where there are competing interests, brothers Jacques (now deceased) and Pierre, and consequently their respective sons, Bertrand and Arnaud, have fallen out, causing a rift in this family success story. Luckily for their fans, the wines are still made. The cool climate and diverse soils of their estate ensure that the wines of Couly-Dutheil remain some of the best Cabernet Franc wines in the world.

The La Coulée sees absolutely no oak fermentation or aging, which allows for the wine to express its fruit flavors purely with no outside influence. Cabernet Franc, in general, is an excellent food pairing wine, with a natural spiciness and intrigue. This wine is no exception, and begs to be enjoyed within a few years of bottling to ensure its naturally bright acidity and flavor. If you want to see Cabernet Franc in its purest form, before it gets beefed up or blended further along on the scale, this is your bottle.

LET'S PAIR IT
Brined Pan-Seared Chicken Breasts with Farro Salad

There are a few schools of thought when pairing wine to food. The first is to match flavors; the second is to match the body of the wine to that of the food; and the third is to match styles. **The pairing of the Couly-Dutheil Chinon with Gabriel's Brined Chicken Breasts with Farro Salad recipe allows us to apply all three theories into one knockout pairing.** The wine—earthy, herbal, peppery—is a perfect match for the herb-brined chicken. Hefty grinds of pepper in the dish give the wine's peppery overtones extra zing, while the unexpected grapes in the earthy farro bring out the wine's purple fruit. But where this pairing really shines is in the perfect matching of styles: rustic, simple, countryside food and wine at its best.

BRINED PAN-SEARED CHICKEN BREASTS
with FARRO SALAD

SERVES 4

**BRINED PAN-SEARED
CHICKEN BREASTS**

4 skin-on, boneless
chicken breasts

Chicken Brine recipe
(see page 109)

Cracked black pepper

Vegetable oil

2 tablespoons butter

2 sprigs rosemary

2 sprigs thyme

2 cloves garlic, smashed

½ lemon

Farro Salad (recipe below)

FARRO SALAD

3 tablespoons extra virgin
olive oil, divided

1 small Spanish onion, diced

½ pound farro

1 quart vegetable or light
chicken stock

Kosher salt and cracked
black pepper

Warm water

¼ bunch broccoli
rabe, chopped

1 tablespoon butter

4 scallions sliced, white
parts only

1 shallot, minced

½ cup red grapes, halved

1 cucumber, peeled
and diced

2 tablespoons
grated pecorino

1 tablespoon toasted
pecans, chopped

1 tablespoon parsley
leaves, chopped

Sherry vinegar to taste

Brining poultry is like an E-ZPass for your bird game; once you make the switch, you'll wonder why you were ever in that other lane. When you brine, your bird is moister, better seasoned, and tastes like it has been bathed in herbs and vegetables—because it has. Most importantly, brining is forgiving. We're all guilty of occasionally overcooking a chicken, but if it's brined, you'll hardly notice. —GABRIEL

Preheat oven to 325°F.

Place chicken breasts in the brine for 30 minutes or up to 2 hours.

Heat a large, heavy-bottomed, ovenproof sauté pan over medium-high heat. Remove the chicken from the brine, pat dry with a paper towel, and season lightly with pepper. Add enough vegetable oil to the pan to coat the bottom. Once the oil is hot, place the breasts, skin-side down, into the pan, making sure they don't crowd one another. Press the meat down with a spatula for 1 minute, to ensure that all of the skin is in contact with the pan. Let the breasts cook undisturbed for at least another 6 to 7 minutes, until the skin is nicely browned. Turn the chicken breasts over and let cook for another 3 minutes. Flip the breasts again and transfer the pan to the oven. Roast until the chicken is cooked through, about 15 to 20 minutes.

Remove the pan from the oven and add the butter, rosemary, thyme, and garlic to the pan. Lightly baste the flesh side of the breasts for 30 seconds or so, and then flip them over and baste the skin side. Squeeze the lemon over the chicken and sauce and then swirl the pan to incorporate. Serve the chicken with the Farro Salad.

FARRO SALAD

Heat a large pot over medium heat, and add 2 tablespoons olive oil. Add the onion and cook for 5 to 6 minutes, until translucent. Add the dry farro and stir until it is evenly coated. Add the stock and season with salt and pepper. Bring the mixture to a boil, then cover and lower the heat. Let simmer for 25 minutes, checking every now and then to add more water as needed. (There should still be liquid in the pot.) Once the farro is tender, strain it, and reserve the cooking liquid. Place the farro on a sheet pan and let cool to room temperature.

Meanwhile, in a medium sauté pan over medium heat, add 1 tablespoon of olive oil and the broccoli rabe. Saute until rabe is just starting to wilt, 2 to 3 minutes, then remove it to a plate and wipe the pan clean. Return pan to

high heat, and let it get very hot. Pull the pan off the heat and carefully add the butter—it will instantly smoke and start to brown. Immediately add the shallots and scallions to the pan and stir to combine. Return the pan to the heat, and add the farro and enough of the reserved cooking liquid to make it easy to toss in the pan. Once the farro is hot, add the sautéed rabe, grape halves, cucumbers, and pecorino, tossing or stirring until well incorporated. Turn off the heat, add the parsley and the pecans, and toss once more in the pan. Add sherry vinegar, salt, and pepper to taste. Serve warm.

ROSÉ WINE

No trend in wine has had a more rocket-like trajectory in the last decade than rosé.
Sales are booming, with everyone from upstart garagistas to iconic domaines making
a rosé. Pictures of pink wine are splashed all over Instagram from April to October.
But misconceptions about rosé abound, so we're here to set the story straight.

Rosé Myth #1

First and foremost, today's rosé wine is not sweet.
Outside of the Millenials, a lot of older wine drinkers
think that rosé is simply a rebranded White Zinfandel for
the hipster generation. Not so. While some rosés express
riper fruit flavors, like watermelon, or have been vinified
with some residual sugar, they are all produced in a dry
style. Meaning, acidity and balance are the hallmarks of
a well-made rosé.

Rosé Myth #2

Rosé is not white wine with a little red wine added in.
This practice of blending red and white wines is actually
frowned upon throughout most of Europe (with an
exception for Champagne).

Rosé Myth #3

Yes, you can drink rosé year round! And yet, rosé
remains seasonal . . . for now. At the moment,
winemakers and distributors control the seasonal
nature of rosé. While it's popular enough that retail
stores and restaurants could sell it all year, there
simply isn't enough quality product to last all twelve
months. So, the market deems spring as the start of
rosé season, and places Thanksgiving as its last gasp.
This ensures there will be a months-long scarcity and
a fever pitch of desire by the time the new vintage
is ready each spring. Like the first sign of tulips and
crocuses, rosé season is our wine reward for surviving
the long winter. But, how is rosé made?

The Saignée Method

Traditionally, rosé was made by the saignée method, a process that "bleeds" off the lighter-colored red wine that is trapped above the must after it is crushed. The sooner the wine is separated from the red grape skins, the lighter in color it is. The lightest rosés are left for just a few hours, while the darker wines have had contact for a few days. This first method of rosé production was functional more than anything, as it allowed for greater concentration of the grape juice underneath the must, leading to a higher quality red wine. The pink juice was fermented in stainless steel and meant to be drunk immediately, usually by the vineyard staff. I'm sure the winemakers who were just trying to avoid waste never thought this wine would become the global phenomenon that it is today!

The Maceration Method

These days, the clamor for rosé wine is so huge that winemakers are earmarking entire vineyards for rosé production, and vinifying the resulting juice only as rosé wine. They designate the whole vat for maceration to their desired color and extraction, and don't just bleed off the top. Every winemaker has his or her own tricks for producing a rosé that suits their label's standards, and while it's not considered the traditional way to produce rosé, volume demands necessitate the change. Some purists say that this isn't real rosé, but, we're too busy drinking it to really care.

CHAPTER 7

WINES WELL WORTH THE EFFORT

If the previous chapter was all about a welcoming, global experience for the American palate, this chapter is the exact opposite. It can take some work to appreciate the wines in this section because they are so very Old World in style, but the reward is worth the effort. We're leaving the lushness of Chapter Six and moving towards more structure and the arrival of grape tannins. We're also starting to see wines that take well to cellar aging, a phenomenon that requires patience and dedication.

5R

ALL STRUCTURE, ALL THE TIME

5R IS, WITHOUT A DOUBT, THE MOST unique section of the entire wine wall at The Urban Grape. Coming as we have from the juiciness of 3R and 4R, you would think that some of those qualities would remain; however, for this chapter, traditional European winemaking techniques that value structure and tannin over juice dominate. In fact, there are very few American wines in our 5R section.

climate	Temperate, mostly sunny climates; many with continued alpine or maritime influence
regions	Tuscany and Sicily, Italy; Rhône Valley and Bordeaux, France; Shenandoah Valley, Virginia; Casablanca, Chile; Rioja, Spain
varietals	Sangiovese, Nero D'Avola, Syrah, Cabernet Sauvignon, Merlot, Cabernet Franc, Carmenere, Tempranillo, Garnacha/Grenache
technique	Longer maceration; oak aging, mostly done in used-oak barrels
characteristics	Structured tannins and a medium body with a mouthfeel resembling whole milk; vibrant acidity; cellar worthy
color	Semi-transparent core with ruby, purple, and garnet hues
ideal pairings	Braised meats; game meats; herbal flavors; earthy vegetables like eggplant and mushrooms; savory dishes

The key word you're going to need to get comfortable with is "structure." Structure begins in earnest here, and it will remain until the end of the Progressive Scale—but what does it mean? Structure is the overall architectural presentation of the wine, but is mostly influenced by acidity and tannins. We know that acidity is important in wine, especially in terms of mouthfeel. But tannins are important, too, and they haven't had a starring role until now.

Tannins come from the grape skin, seeds, and stems that are still present during the maceration and fermentation of red wine. Their purpose, among other things, is to add texture and complexity. Charlotte couldn't have built her web without the barn beams around her, and tannins provide those same types of building blocks. They're noticeable to us because they are sticky in our mouth, and create a dragging sensation like corduroy pants on a velvet couch. So, even though tannins are what make a wine stand up to a meal, or what help a wine keep its structure while it's aging, they can be a little off-putting until you're used to that sensation.

The European and European-style wines in 5R can really feel like a departure from our earlier, "yummy" wines, but they're an important gateway into what comes next, when wines start showing all of these elements in balanced form. 5R wines are the wines against which the newer style wines are judged, because the most famous, classic wines are in this section: Bordeaux, Rioja, Barolo, Chianti, and Barbaresco, among others. Drinking them may feel more challenging, but to ignore them is to ignore the history of wine, and the foundation upon which all modern winemaking has been built. Moderate aging and pairing the wines with the right food will help make them more approachable.

GEEKOUT: ESTERS — WHY WINE CAN SMELL LIKE RASPBERRIES

Ready for some chemistry? Esters are compounds that are made when an acid and an alcohol react and eliminate a molecule of water. Fragrance esters are incredibly recognizable to us, and conjure up vivid memories of time, place, and experience. Fresh cut grass, bacon frying, tomato plants in the summer sun: These are just some of the vivid aromas that we can all recognize immediately.

When acid and alcohol react during winemaking, aromatic esters in the grape are released. Fermentation magnifies these smells, with some grape varietals displaying smells more intensely than others. With the presence of so many esters it can be hard for our brains (which are used to smelling one thing at a time) to pull apart the tangle of smells in our wine glasses, which is why part of learning about wine is learning how to tease out the leading aromas.

It's not cheating to learn the common esters, or aromas, of the leading grape varietals. On the contrary, it will help your brain get organized if you know what you're "supposed" to be smelling. But once you've figured out what to expect, stick your nose back in the glass and see if you can pull out some other aromas. You'll be amazed to find that so much of tasting wine actually comes from smelling it.

Our Favorite Regions and Varietals

We know we've just talked about how the 5R wines are less approachable than their neighbors in 3R and 4R, but we don't want to scare you off from exploring this section. Given time to aerate, and paired with the right food, these wines are spectacular. Think of them as you would Brussels sprouts. Maybe a little weird on their own, but sautéed in butter and served with bacon, there's nothing more sublime.

UNITED STATES

REGION: Virginia
VARIETAL: Cabernet Franc

Wine aficionados need new challenges, and our latest challenge is Virginia. I would be lying if I said any of us at UG are Virginia wine experts, but we're intrigued and we're learning. Virginian winemakers seem to have gotten a handle on what grows best in their state, and one of their thriving medium-bodied varietals is Cabernet Franc. Petit Verdot and the historic American varietal, Norton, also grow well in the state. All are medium-bodied and exhibit nice structure and fruit. Virginia is actively wooing wine lovers to visit and explore their seven AVAs. A trip to Europe or Napa may feel out-of-reach, but you'll learn just as much during a drive through Virginia.

SPAIN

REGION: Rioja
VARIETALS: Tempranillo, Garnacha

Rioja is one of the oldest winemaking regions in the modern world, and continues to dominate the international wine scene with their use of structured grape varieties, like Tempranillo and Garnacha, and their finely tuned use of oak aging. Rioja has mastered the even-handed use of oak to soften the prickly edges of their varietals, and the resulting wines are food- and palate-friendly. They also employ lengthy barrel and bottle aging, so don't be surprised if the current vintage is almost a decade old. A well-made wine will keep its fruit as it ages, so make sure you choose a quality producer. Riojas need time to open up, but what they lose in pop-and-pour ability, they make up for in general wine dominance.

FRANCE

REGION: Bordeaux
VARIETALS: Cabernet Sauvignon, Merlot, Cabernet Franc, Malbec, Petit Verdot

Here it is, the big daddy of the wine world: Bordeaux. Although they show up from 4R to 6R, we love medium-bodied Bordeaux wines. The cornerstone of Bordeaux is the region's innovative blending of five red varietals: Cabernet Sauvignon, Merlot, Cabernet Franc, Malbec, and Petit Verdot. The region's main influence is the system of river beds and estuaries that come off the Gironde, Garonne, and Dordogne rivers, and form the "Left Bank" and "Right Bank" of Bordeaux. The Left Bank primarily uses Cabernet Sauvignon as its base for blending, while the Right Bank prefers Merlot. Bordeaux wine prices can be astronomical, but one can find affordable wines, especially from the Left Bank. Look for second labels from well-respected houses, or ask your wine shop for a lesser-known producer.

WHAT TO EAT WITH
— 5R WINES —

5R wines not only need food, but benefit greatly from the right food pairing.
The difference between 5R wines and the ones that came before them is
structure. An increase in tannins makes these wines feel drier and less fruity.
Add in pronounced acidity, and you have a beautifully made wine, but one
that really needs food to show all its nuances.

WHEN IN DOUBT, MAKE RISOTTO

6 cups broth

1 tablespoon olive oil

2 tablespoons butter, divided

1 small onion, chopped

1 ½ cups Arborio rice

1 cup wine (white is more traditional, but it's ok to use red as well)

½ cup Parmesan cheese

Risotto is the perfect meal to make when you have odds and ends in your fridge that don't really add up to their own meal. We're particularly fond of risotto made with traditional Italian ingredients—although, truth be told we've never met a risotto we didn't like. One of our favorite combinations is risotto with mushrooms and peas, a dish that pairs perfectly with the earthy, structured nuances of the wines in the 5R section.

Heat the broth over low heat. In a straight-sided sauté pan, heat the olive oil and 1 tablespoon butter. Add onions and cook until tender. Add in the Arborio rice and stir for 1 minute to toast the grains. Add the wine, and stir until fully incorporated. Add in the broth, a ladle full at a time, and stir after each addition until the liquid is absorbed. This should take about 15 minutes. When the rice is al dente, add in remaining butter, Parmesan cheese, and half a ladle of broth. Stir to combine off heat.

For mushroom and pea risotto: Heat butter and olive oil in a sauté pan, and add a variety of mushrooms in a single layer. Season with salt and pepper and don't touch them. Don't even look at them! Only when they have started to release some water and are browned on the bottom can you stir in some chopped thyme and let them cook for a couple more minutes. Add them into the risotto, along with the peas (frozen are fine), when you stir in the last of the broth, butter, and cheese.

PERFECT PAIRINGS

Savory dishes

·············

Herbal flavors

·············

Earthy vegetables like mushrooms and eggplant

·············

Braised meats

·············

Game meats

FOODS TO AVOID

Shellfish

ONE TO TRY

CASTELLO ROMITORIO ROSSO DI MONTALCINO (TUSCANY, ITALY)

ONE DAY IN ITALY, A GROUP OF thirteen of us, aged 3 to 73, drove up the narrow switchbacks of Montalcino, going higher and higher until we hit the literal end of the road. We doubled back a mile until we saw our destination: an endless driveway lined with cypress trees, leading our cars to Castello Romitorio.

Once a fortress, and then a monastery, Castello Romitorio was abandoned in the 1950s and fell into disrepair. There are many amazing stories from the Castello's history, but our favorite was one we heard while gazing across the valley to a distant fortress on the next peak, and heard about the secret tunnel that connects the two. You know all the kids in our group begged to explore that forgotten connector!

The Castello stayed vacant until the early 1980s, when renowned Italian artist, and Andy Warhol contemporary, Sandro Chia bought the property and began restoring the Castello and installing vineyards around the monastery. The farmers below him thought he was crazy for trying to grow Tuscany's varietals at that high of an altitude. Little did they know that he was about to open one of the finest wineries in the region.

The grounds of the estate are decorated with Sandro's sculptures, the most intriguing of which is the giant *Cinghiale* (wild boar) that stands protectively on the roof of the estate's cellars. The buildings on the grounds, no matter how functional, are graced with Sandro's paintings, as are the wine labels on all of their bottles. Bold, masculine, and vibrant, the paintings are perfectly representative of what the bottles hold: traditional Italian wines made to express the very best of the region.

Our group of thirteen toured the facilities, peeked through the keyhole of the Castello (now Sandro's home), and were treated to an expertly, yet simply prepared, traditional meal, paired with the estate's wines. From white to rosé and through their many reds, there wasn't a misstep among the bottles. We sell case after case of the Romitorio wines that we are able to get in Boston, but the enduring customer favorite is their Rosso di Montalcino. Made from 100 percent Sangiovese Grosso, this wine has a youthful quality to it, despite being aged one year in oak and three to five years in bottle before it is released. The bottle aging helps to tame the natural astringency and structure of the Sangiovese, bringing out its richness and beauty. It's a perfect food wine—and a regular reminder of a glorious day spent at the tippy tippy top of Montalcino.

LET'S PAIR IT
Braised Pork Shanks with Beans and Breadcrumb Salsa

There are some pairings that work so exceptionally well that it's almost impossible to tease out why. **The Castello Romitorio Rosso, at heart a rustic wine, and Braised Pork Shanks with Beans, at heart a rustic meal, is one of those exceptional pairings.** On paper the pairing works because the high acid Sangiovese grape makes wine that cuts through rich food. In return, the rich meal mellows out the structure of the wine, and makes it fruitier and sweeter. But on an emotional level, this pairing works because it is a modern day version of what Italians have been eating and drinking for hundreds of years: a simple, soulful, and hyper-local pairing.

BRAISED PORK SHANKS
with BEANS AND BREADCRUMB SALSA

SERVES 4

BRAISED PORK SHANKS

4 pork shanks (about 6 pounds, total)

Kosher salt and black pepper

¼ cup canola oil

2 Spanish onions, roughly diced

2 carrots, roughly diced

1 stalk celery, roughly diced

3 cloves garlic, smashed

1 tablespoon tomato paste

1 cup white wine

4 cups chicken stock

1 thick slice of slab bacon (optional)

4 sprigs thyme

2 sprigs rosemary

1 bay leaf

DRY AND FRESH BEANS

¼ pound green beans

1 teaspoon extra virgin olive oil

Kosher salt and cracked black pepper

2 tablespoons butter

2 shallots, thinly sliced

1 clove garlic, sliced

2 scallions, sliced, greens and all

4 cups cooked or canned beans

2 tablespoons parsley leaves

Squeeze of lemon

BREADCRUMB SALSA

1 shallot, minced

1 tablespoon chopped capers

½ cup parsley, chopped

Zest of 1 lemon

1 tablespoon champagne or white wine vinegar

1 teaspoon anchovy paste

½ cup extra virgin olive oil

¼ cup coarse breadcrumbs, toasted

Sea salt and cracked black pepper

Pork shanks can be hard to locate unless you have a local butcher. If so, call and place an order in advance. If not, substitute the shanks with a 4- to 5-pound pork shoulder. The bacon in this recipe is optional, but soooo worth it. For the beans, I'd love for you to buy some great dried beans—like those from a local farmers' market or from Rancho Gordo, which you would soak, and then cook, by covering with water, and adding mire poix, garlic, and herbs, for a good 1 to 1 ½ hours—but good quality canned beans, like a mix of cannellini and black-eyed peas, will work, too. —GABRIEL

Season the shanks liberally with salt and black pepper. Place a medium braising pot over high heat, and then after a minute or two, add the canola oil. Once the oil is smoking add the shanks. Brown them on all sides, about 8 to 10 minutes. Place browned shanks on a plate. Turn the heat to medium-low and add the onions, carrots, and celery, waiting 1 minute between each; stir the mixture every so often for about 5 minutes. When the vegetables begin to soften, add the garlic and the tomato paste and let toast for 1 minute. Add the wine, and after 1 minute, add the chicken stock and bring it just to a boil. Add the bacon, herbs, and shanks. Turn the heat down to low and cover the pan. Cook for at least 2 hours, until the meat is very tender and starting to fall off the bone. Carefully remove the shanks to a plate and tent with foil. Strain the liquid, pressing hard on any solids to make sure that you get as much liquid as possible out. Put the strained sauce back in the braising pot and raise heat to medium. Reduce the sauce by roughly half, until it begins to thicken.

Serve the shanks over the Dry and Fresh Beans, generously ladling sauce over the shanks and beans. Top with Breadcrumb Salsa.

DRY AND FRESH BEANS

Toss the green beans in a bowl with the olive oil and season with salt and pepper. Heat a cast iron skillet over high heat. Once hot, add green beans and let sear for 1 minute or until they just start to blister and blacken. Remove the green beans and reserve. Add the butter and let it begin to brown. As soon as it does, add the shallots, garlic, and scallions, and let them almost begin to brown, about 30 seconds to 1 minute. Add the 4 cups of cooked beans. Once the cooked beans are heated through, add the green beans, parsley, and lemon juice. Toss and adjust the seasoning. Serve immediately.

BREADCRUMB SALSA

Combine all ingredients in a medium bowl. Season to taste with salt and pepper.

EMBRACING THE BLENDS

THIS SECTION USHERS IN ONE OF THE most exciting—and often misunderstood—aspects of winemaking: blending! Blending is a post-fermentation technique that combines juice made from different grape varietals into one seamless wine. Many varietals, like Pinot Noir, Gamay, and Mencia, are known for almost always being single varietal wines, with one exception: Pinot Noir is often blended with Chardonnay to make Champagne or sparkling wine. The final products are often made by combining the juice of different vineyard sites, but not different varietals. Red blends,

climate	Primarily warmer climates; a few cooler climate regions that see more manipulation
regions	Piedmont and Tuscany, Italy; Rioja, Spain; Chateauneuf-du-Pape and St. Joseph, France; Douro Valley and Alentejo, Portugal
varietals	Nebbiolo, Sangiovese, Tempranillo, Cabernet Sauvignon, Grenache, Syrah, Mourvèdre, Touriga Nacional, Aragonez
technique	A variety of longer-period, oak-aging techniques; some regions blend wine to achieve desired result
characteristics	Structured but balanced tannins; a mouthfeel of whole-milk-plus; palate-friendly and cellar-worthy
color	Semi-opaque ruby, garnet, purple, and black tones
ideal pairings	Grilled meats; charred vegetables; wild boar; pasta and risotto; lobster

on the other hand, take the emphasis off that single varietal, and instead focus on producing a pleasurable, well-rounded drinking experience.

Red wine blending does happen earlier in the Progressive Scale, with the most famous example, of course, being Bordeaux and its blend of five different varietals: Cabernet Sauvignon, Merlot, Petit Verdot, Cabernet Franc, and Malbec. But 6R is when the blend that defines the Rhône Valley—Grenache, Syrah, and Mourvèdre—gains dominance, and the popularity of the region's wine influences winemaking for the rest of the Progressive Scale.

The goal of blending at this stage is to soften the tannins and acidity of these structured varietals. By combining varietals with varied characteristics, the winemakers are able to adjust the profile of the finished wine. The end game is balance in aroma, color, fruit, spiciness, structure, and finish. Because the wines have been combined with others, they are often approachable and palate-friendly, while maintaining structure.

For a long time, people felt like blends outside of Bordeaux and the Rhône were a cop-out, a way for a winemaker to hide flaws in the vintage or winemaking. But more and more, blends are gaining acceptance, and are being recognized as some of the most approachable wines on the market. Here's how we look at blended wine: A perfect tomato is just that, *perfect*. It needs literally nothing else added to it to delight your senses. But that doesn't mean that a perfect tomato can't be turned into an equally delightful tomato sauce by adding a few more ingredients. The same is true with wine. So, go ahead: play around with blends. Experiment first with the famously delicious Rhône Valley blends, and then expand from there to understand what blends appeal the most to your palate.

GEEKOUT:
WHEN TO DECANT WINE

There's a lot of debate about the benefits of decanting. Some people say all wine should be decanted; others think this is blasphemy. We're somewhere in the middle. Decanting wine, which is moving the wine from the bottle in to another vessel to allow oxygenation, is vital for structured wines, like the ones we've talked about in this chapter. If you have time, go for a full decant. If not, run your wine through an aerator as you pour it. Adding any amount of oxygen into the wine, even just by swirling the wine in your glass, will allow for more immediate drinking pleasure.

Decanting is also important for wines that have a lot of sediment in them. No one wants to swallow a mouthful of grit! Pros like TJ, who've decanted lots of bottles, can separate the wine from the sediment with careful pouring. If you have a steady hand, try it. Otherwise, carefully pour the wine through a wine strainer or cheesecloth to catch any sediment that sneaks out. Decanting also helps age-worthy wines that aren't quite ready for drinking because the oxygen helps smooth out the nervous edges. In short, decant anything that comes across as a little tight right out of the bottle.

That said, a lot of the wine sold today is meant to be popped and poured. Most white wines and many of the lighter-bodied reds don't need any decanting at all. The best way to develop your decanting sixth sense is to play around with it: Taste the wine when it's first opened, then taste again after passing a glass through an aerator, then taste *again* once you've poured it into a decanter. Soon, you'll know just what and how to decant.

6R Our Favorite Regions and Varietals

This section of the wine wall is home to some of the most famous regions and varietals in the world. They are renowned for their history, the structure that enhances their age-worthiness, and their ability to elevate simple meals into an occasion. If you're a novice wine drinker, you may find their structure (and, often, price point) intimidating, but before long you'll be craving these serious wines in your glass.

FRANCE

REGION: Southern Rhône
VARIETALS: Grenache, Syrah, Mourvèdre

The southern Rhône Valley is an influential and popular stretch of French winemaking territory, known for its juicy, food-friendly wines. These wines are generally less structured and more approachable than others in this section. We love the region's signature red wine blend of Grenache, Syrah, and Mourvèdre, or "GSM." This blend is so popular that regions around the world use the technique, but perhaps none is more famous than France's Châteauneuf-du-Pape AOC. The blend typically starts with Grenache, the lightest-bodied and highest-toned of the bunch. Next comes Syrah, with purple fruit flavors and black olive earthiness. The blend is finished off with Mourvèdre, which adds richness, tannins, and a long finish. Layered fruit, bright acidity, tannic structure, and salty earthiness—a perfect blend!

ITALY

REGION: Piedmont
VARIETAL: Nebbiolo

We're back up in Piedmont again to talk about Nebbiolo (again), this time made in one of the most famous Italian wine regions, Barolo. The hillside vineyards of Barolo sit higher than the other Nebbiolo-growing areas and receive more sun exposure throughout the day. The resulting fully ripened grapes account for Barolo's fuller body and richer flavor. Barolo wines need long stretches of barrel aging—by law three years minimum—to soften their strident tannins and high acidity, and usually need time in your cellar after that. But they're worth the wait—as a food pairing wine, there are few better. If you want to experience Barolo, but want fewer challenges, try Barbaresco, which produces wines that are as age-worthy as Barolo, but feminine in style and more approachable.

PORTUGAL

REGION: Alentejo
VARIETALS: Aragonez, Trincadeira, Alicante Bouchet, Syrah, Cabernet Sauvignon

The indigenous red grapes of Portugal—Aragonez (Tempranillo), Trincadeira, Alicante Bouchet, to name a few—are difficult to pronounce and spell, and finding them stateside can be hard. The region of Alentejo covers about a third of the country, and, along with Vinho Verde, is responsible for producing the most popular and widely exported wines from Portugal. The region is known for blended red wines that are, generally speaking, medium-bodied, quite drinkable, and reasonably priced, especially in comparison to more famous wine regions. Try wines blended with all indigenous grapes, or choose a blend featuring a better-known grape like Syrah or Cabernet Sauvignon.

WHAT TO EAT WITH
— 6R WINES —

The wines in the 6R section are regionally influenced, *and truly meant to pair with each area's most famous main course meals. If you're ever stuck wondering what to pair, a medium-bodied red wine paired with a traditional, regional meal is always a safe bet. The blended wines in this section help to make the wines more palate-friendly than 5R, but structure remains in the forefront.*

BABA'S PASTA SAUCE

½ cup olive oil

6-8 cloves garlic, finely minced

Two 28-ounce cans crushed tomatoes (San Marzano, if possible)

28 ounces of water

⅓ cup finely chopped parsley (about half a bunch)

1 tablespoon dried oregano

1 tablespoon dried basil

1 teaspoon salt

½ teaspoon pepper

1 teaspoon sugar (optional)

1 pound ground beef

There is one meal that will set our children into wild squeals of anticipation: Baba's Pasta Sauce. My mother (aka: Baba, to her grandchildren) may be of Scottish heritage, but her bright and tomato-y sauce with big chunks of ground beef brings out her Italian nonna. The richness of the sauce and meat and the sturdiness of the pasta make for a nice pairing for the structure and body of 6R wines.

In a large saucepan, gently warm the olive oil until fragrant. Add the garlic, and stir continuously for 30 seconds. Add tomatoes. Fill each empty tomato can halfway up with the water and swirl to rinse, dumping the water and tomato remnants into the pot. Add the remaining ingredients through the sugar, if you choose to add it.

Bring to a boil and immediately reduce heat. Simmer for 1 to 2 hours, until the sauce is thickened. I use an immersion blender on my sauce to make it smooth; my mother does not. Your choice! Adjust the seasonings. The sauce will surely need additional salt, but add it at the end.

Place the ground beef in a large sauté pan, and cook over moderately high heat until cooked all the way through. Season with salt and pepper, strain the grease, and add the meat to the sauce. If you have time, simmer the sauce and meat together for 30 minutes. Serve over your favorite pasta with lots of Parmesan cheese.

PERFECT PAIRINGS

Grilled meats

Charred vegetables

Famous regional dishes

Wild boar

Pasta and risotto

Lobster

FOODS TO AVOID

Summer fruits

ONE TO TRY

BODEGAS MUGA "RESERVA" (RIOJA, SPAIN)

THERE ARE A LOT OF PERKS TO OUR job (free wine being among the best of them), but one of the most life-affirming aspects has to be the incredible people that we meet from winemaking countries all around the world. Often, we find ourselves at a dinner table with strangers, our shared passion for wine the only ice breaker we need.

Of all the dinners we've been to, several have been truly transformative. Our cold winter night out with Manu Muga at a cozy restaurant in Newton, Massachusetts, stands out as the moment that we became passionate about Rioja. There was no way to resist his stories about the region, nor the wines themselves. Our horizons were broadened that night and we, and our palates, are forever thankful.

Along with his brothers, Manu is a third-generation steward of his family's vineyard. What Manu's grandfather started in 1932 has grown steadily in both acreage and acclaim. Along the way, Bodegas Muga has revolutionized and modernized winemaking in Spain's Rioja appellation, all while producing wines that recall the most traditional and historical aspects of the region.

Bodegas Muga has a way with oak. Winemakers who want to learn how to use oak with a steady and efficient hand should be required to spend time under their tutelage. Oak runs through everything they do. They operate their own barrel-making cooperage, with at least three barrel-makers and one master cooper on the payroll. They maintain 14,000 oak barrels made out of three types of French wood, as well as American, Hungarian, Russian, and Spanish oak. Despite the fact that all of their wines see oak, not even the most oak-sensitive palate would complain. That's how well-integrated the wood is into the rest of the wines' structure.

Muga is known for its red wines, but the white, rosé, and Cava wines are also extraordinary, as well as more affordable than some of the higher-end red wines. The Reserva is primarily Tempranillo, mixed with Garnacha, Mazuelo, and Graciano. Like most of the more structured wines we see in 6R, it's aged for 24 months in barrel and 12 months in bottle before being released. Even then, the gripping tannins benefit from time lying in a cellar to mellow with age.

The wines from Bodegas Muga will keep you coming back again and again. And thanks to our night out with Manu we have two birth year magnums from Muga aging in our wine cellar, waiting to be enjoyed with our sons when the time is right.

LET'S PAIR IT
A Clam Bake

One of Gabriel's requests for this book was that we consider pairing a red wine with a seafood recipe that has been served at Straight Wharf for years. We were skeptical but intrigued, and he was right. **When we finally tasted the Bodegas Muga Reserva and the Clam Bake together, we knew immediately that it was an exceptional pairing.** This meal is sweet, rich, salty, creamy, and powerful. The Muga cuts through the mouth smorgasbord and lets each flavor shine on its own. But this whole experience hinges on the pairing of chorizo and red wine from the Rioja region—a classic regional pairing that shines through in each bite.

**SERVES 4
AS AN APPETIZER**

4 ears of corn

1 onion, halved and peeled

4 sprigs basil

6 sprigs parsley

2 sprigs thyme

8 tablespoons butter, divided

2 leeks, cleaned

2 sticks spicy chorizo

Champagne vinegar

1 shallot, minced

20 littleneck clams, washed

1 cup white wine

8 fingerling potatoes

1 clove garlic

1 sprig rosemary

2 tablespoons extra virgin
olive oil

Two 1½-pound lobsters,
meat cooked and
removed from the shell

A CLAM BAKE

This is a more refined version of a clam bake—one that might seem daunting but is well worth the effort, especially if you love the romance of a meal on the beach without, you know, like, sand and shells. Ask a fishmonger for cooked lobster meat, which will cut down significantly on the work. —GABRIEL

Using a serrated knife, cut the kernels from the corn cobs, reserving both. Place the cobs in a large pot with one half of the onion, plus the basil, parsley, and thyme. Cover the cobs just barely with cold water and bring to a boil over high heat. Reduce heat to a simmer and cook, uncovered, for 30 minutes or until only 1 to 2 cups of liquid remain. Strain mixture through a fine-mesh strainer, reserving the liquid. Discard the cobs and herbs.

In a medium saucepan over low heat, heat 4 tablespoons of the butter and add the corn kernels. Cook until bright yellow, and then add the strained corn stock until it just covers the kernels. Cook until the mixture is almost dry and then remove from heat. In small batches, puree the corn mixture in a blender until smooth. Pass mixture through a fine-mesh strainer and return it to the pan to keep warm.

Slice the cleaned leeks into rings, about ¼-inch thick. Blanch them in boiling, salted water until tender, about 45 seconds; immediately remove them and shock them in an ice bath. Once cool, remove the leeks from the ice bath and pat dry. Set aside.

Slice the chorizo into ¼-inch thick rings. Place the chorizo ends and scraps into a small pot over low heat and render the fat, making sure not to burn it. Once rendered, strain the chorizo and reserve the fat. To make the chorizo vinaigrette, add half as much champagne vinegar as there is chorizo fat to the pot, as well as the minced shallot; whisk until incorporated. Let cool to room temperature.

Slice the remaining half onion. In a large sauté pan over medium heat, melt 1 tablespoon of butter and sweat the onion until translucent; add the clams and 1 cup white wine. Cover the pan and cook until the clams start to open, about 2 minutes. Once they've opened, immediately remove the clams and spread them out on a sheet pan. Once they are cool enough to handle, remove the meat from the shells and set aside; discard the shells.

Preheat oven to 450°F and place a sheet pan on the center rack. Put the fingerling potatoes, the garlic, and the rosemary into a small pot and cover with salted cold water. Bring to a boil, then remove from heat and cover

the pan; let sit for 20 minutes. Strain the potatoes and then slice them into quarters. Toss them in a bowl with the olive oil, and then throw them on the pre-heated sheet pan and return them to the oven, cooking until they begin to get golden and crispy, about 15 minutes. Remove them from the oven and set them aside.

To assemble the dish: Preheat oven to 350°F. Barely melt the remaining butter in a small pot or microwave. Slice the lobster tail meat in half and place the tail meat, plus the meat from the four claws, into a baking dish in a single layer, and then brush the meat with the melted butter. Cook in the oven until the meat is barely heated through, about 5 to 6 minutes. In a large sauté pan over medium heat, cook the sliced chorizo until hot and crispy, about 2 minutes per side. Add the potatoes, leeks, and clam meat and combine. Cook until heated through. To serve, spoon a small amount of the warm corn fondue onto the center of the plate, and top with some of the chorizo and clam mixture. Place half a tail and a claw on top of each plated mixture. Garnish with a drizzle of the chorizo vinaigrette around the corn fondue.

JUDGING A BOOK BY ITS COVER

We've spent all this time trying to understand what's inside the bottle, but we can't forget the package itself. Undoubtedly the hardest part of any wine buying experience is understanding the wine itself. However, interpreting what the wine label is trying to tell you is half the battle in choosing a wine that fits your needs.

Where to Start

For most shoppers, it's best to start by looking at the region and varietal. Remember that if you don't see the varietal listed on the front (i.e. Sauvignon Blanc), then the region will give you the next biggest hint as to what's in the bottle. Many Old World producers will only list the region, expecting you to know their designated varietals (i.e. a white Sancerre is *always* Sauvignon Blanc). For Old World wines, the sooner you learn which varietals are grown in each region, the easier your life will be. And even then, there will be exceptions.

Who to Trust

Next, it's time to evaluate the producer and the importer. As a general rule, if we've seen a wine label on the side of a truck, a magazine ad, or a billboard, we keep moving. Seek out the more unique producers and you'll be rewarded for your effort. Lots of people shop by importer and that's ok! Quality importers find the best of the best and do the investigative work for you. If you

notice you love the wines of a certain importer, it makes your life much easier to seek out their bottles first. Neal Rosenthal, Kermit Lynch, Terry Theise, Leonardo LoCascio, Michael Skurnik, and Jorge Ordoñez are some of the most reputable importer names.

The Numbers

Yes, the numbers on the label do matter, and your next step is to evaluate the vintage and the alcohol by volume (ABV). These days, winemakers are often able to correct for wet weather or a shorter growing season during production—but it's simply a truth that some vintages are better than others. While keeping abreast of vintage projections is important, don't let it rule you. The wine press lamented that the entire California 2011 vintage was ruined by rain, but we find that the wines are actually quite appealing.

ABV influences the body of the wine, as well as the experience with your food pairing. If you are having

something spicy for dinner, you won't want to grab a high ABV wine because spice + high alcohol = flaming mouth. As a general rule, the richer your meal is, the higher ABV your wine can be.

Additional Information

As you learn more about wine, there are other clues on the label that will matter to you. The most important is probably whether a wine is "Estate Bottled." This means that all the fruit was grown on vineyards owned or farmed by the producers. Often, these wines are considered higher quality because one entity has had total control of the process, start to finish. Along those lines, "Single Vineyard" takes it one step further, and indicates that the wine in that bottle came from one specific vineyard site. Producers make these wines to express the specific terroir(s) of the vineyard.

If you are sensitive to sulfites, you'll want to look for clues about added sulfites on the back label. Most bottles say "Contains Sulfites" or "No Added Sulfites," but remember, all wine contains some sulfites that were produced during fermentation. Many back labels also tell a little story about the wine—so, go ahead and turn that bottle over to see if you're intrigued.

Judge That Book

The look of the label matters. Quality producers take the time to make their labels jump off the shelves. If it catches your eye, pick the bottle up and learn a little more about it. Your experience with that wine starts the second you notice and touch the bottle. If you hate the label your wine might languish on your counter, unopened—and we'd never want that. However, don't be scared of the old-fashioned European labels. A lot of the best producers simply refuse to modernize the look of their labels, and when you've been making quality wine for generations, who are we to judge?

CHAPTER 8

IT IS POSSIBLE TO HAVE IT ALL

We started with red wines that had acid, and, in the next chapter, we added juice. After that, we transitioned to intense structure. Chapter Eight is where we start to put all of the elements together for our wine drinking pleasure. These wines have balanced acid, juice, tannins, and structure. And while everything is coalescing, we're not yet at the top of the Progressive Scale, so these wines are still inherently food- and palate-friendly. For most of our customers, 7R and 8R are happy stops on the wine trail.

7R

WHERE OLD MEETS NEW (THE SEQUEL)

YOU MAY REMEMBER THAT 7W focused on the intersection of Old World and New World characteristics in white wine. For one glorious moment in that section, the world's winemaking techniques converge to produce white wines that all palates can enjoy. The same synergy happens for red wines in 7R, resulting in wines that are almost universally acclaimed and blissfully palate-friendly.

AT A GLANCE

climate	Drier, warmer climates with more influence from the sun
regions	Napa Valley and Sonoma County, California; Columbia Valley, Washington; Bandol, France; Ribera del Duero, Spain; Mendoza, Argentina; Puglia, Italy
varietals	Zinfandel, Cabernet Sauvignon, Merlot, Syrah, Mourvèdre, Malbec, Negroamaro
technique	Longer maceration; barrel fermentation; more frequent new-barrel-oak aging
characteristics	Fuller bodied with a mouthfeel of half-and-half; palate-friendly, bold with ripe fruit and softer tannins
color	Mostly opaque burgundy with garnet and plum tones
ideal pairings	Red meat; stews; herbs; Mediterranean flavors; Indian spices; high-acid foods

7R wines are a lot like 3R wines, but they have more of everything: more sun, more juice, more maceration, more alcohol, more wood, more aging, and more yumminess. All of that adds up to more full-bodied wines. While Bordeaux is fading in prominence by 7R, the Bordeaux varietals (among them, Cabernet Sauvignon, Merlot, Cabernet Franc, Malbec, Carmenere, and Petit Verdot) from other regions across the world are bursting on to the scene. These wines are grown in warmer, but not yet hot, climates in California, Washington State, South Africa, South America, and regions in France like the Rhône Valley. The spread of Bordeaux varietals to other regions around the world is one of the major influences on modern red winemaking. Old world-style Syrah, Zinfandel, and Primitivo also shine in 7R.

Historically, California Cabernet Sauvignon was made in a more Old World style, with shorter maceration times for less intense flavor and color, lower alcohol, and more tempered wood treatments. That style fell out of favor in the late '90s when California winemakers went for as much flavor and boldness as possible. But the pendulum has started to swing back toward moderation and the best "new" Cali Cabs, which we find in 7R, are made in a more traditional "old" style, often using stainless steel and concrete in the process to lessen the effects of the wood barrels on the wine.

Because these wines are so universally palate-friendly, they make the ultimate dinner party wines. They're juicy enough to taste great without food, but are structured and tannic enough to make a nice pairing for just about anything on your plate. While they're serious wines, they don't take themselves too seriously, which means you'll be intrigued by what's in your glass without having to think about it too much!

GEEKOUT: WINE ALLERGIES

"I can't drink red wine, it gives me a headache" is a heartbreakingly common refrain, and one that is two times more likely to be uttered by a woman. Wine allergies are a sad, but real, thing and are not just caused by over-indulgence. That said, let's start with over-indulgence. We recommend the 1:1 rule for drinking wine. For every glass of alcohol, have a glass of water. That usually mitigates all non-allergy related headaches. If you're still getting a headache, it may signal an allergy.

In terms of allergies, the least serious symptom is flushing. We all get a little flushed when we drink, but people with mild allergies get hives or a rosacea-like rash, probably as a reaction to the ethanol in alcohol. Yet, we know plenty of people that will still enjoy a glass of wine, even if it means turning red. Things get more serious when a glass of wine causes respiratory issues like wheezing or shortness of breath. That usually signals an allergic reaction to the sulfites in wine. In these cases, you might try a dry white wine or a "no sulfites added" red wine, which won't have additional sulfites added as a preservative. But escaping sulfites in wine altogether is difficult, no matter what the wine marketing experts might say.

Lastly, there are those who get headaches. The likely culprit is histamines, which are found in the skin of the grape, making red wine more of an issue than white. There are red grape varietals like Barbera and Dolcetto that have less histamines in the skin, which, anecdotally anyway, cause less of an allergic reaction. But the reality may be that for some, red wine is off the table.

Our Favorite Regions and Varietals

The intersection of Old World and New World means there's a little something for everyone in this section. Bordeaux may be fading, but the Bordeaux varietals are just getting started.

UNITED STATES

REGION: Yakima Valley, Washington
VARIETAL: Merlot

Yakima Valley was the first winegrowing appellation to be established in the Pacific Northwest in 1983, and is Washington's largest and best-known winemaking region. As regions go, this one is still a baby, but not the youngest in America. (There are new AVAs being created all the time!) Bordeaux varietals do extremely well in Washington, particularly the region's masculine and well-balanced Merlot. The grape grows well in Washington because the relatively dry climate allows for more even and balanced ripening. Merlot is still battling the damage inflicted to its reputation by over-production—and the movie *Sideways*—but a come-back is on the horizon, and it's worth seeking out as a delicious food pairing wine.

UNITED STATES

REGION: Sonoma County, California
VARIETAL: Cabernet Sauvignon

Alexander Valley, the largest of Sonoma's AVAs, is located in the heart of the Russian River Valley in California. While most of Sonoma is influenced by the Pacific Ocean, Alexander Valley is shielded on its west side by a range of hills. As a result, the temperature is more consistently warm than other Sonoma appellations, which results in perfectly ripened (but not overly ripe) grapes. The Alexander Valley winemakers believe that the mineral deposits from the Russian River closely resemble those in Bordeaux, and, as a result, Cabernet Sauvignon is a top dog in the region. Napa may get all the fame for its Cabernet Sauvignon, but the wines from this region win points from us for having a more restrained, Old World style.

ITALY

REGION: Puglia
VARIETAL: Negroamaro

Tuscany may be Italy's best-known wine region, but Puglia (found in Italy's boot) is the workhorse, and one of the highest wine production areas in the country. Salice Salentino is our favorite appellation and makes excellent and affordable wines from the Negroamaro grape. Fun to say and even more fun to drink, Negroamaro has a deep, rich color, and beautiful aromatics and flavors. There is some dispute over the correct translation of the name: Some believe it breaks down to "black" and "bitter," while others believe a Latin influence translates both word roots to "black." Either way, while the grape does produce structured tannins, the abundant purple fruit flavors overcome any mild bitterness and make this wine one of the most effortless to drink—some might even say chuggable!

WHAT TO EAT WITH
— 7R WINES —

We're back to yummy wines, although the 7R wines have more concentration and body than their younger siblings in 3R. But we also still have structure and nuance, which makes the wines in this section some of the most well-balanced for the American palate. There's often an Old World influence on these wines, so, turning to traditional flavors is a good idea for wine pairing. These wines can also handle spice, making them a great take out pairing, too.

TACO TUESDAY

Over the years, we've noticed that if we roll a new food into a corn tortilla and call it a taco, our kids will eat it without complaint. Needless to say, Taco Tuesday—both homemade and take-out—happens every week in our house.

In the summer, we love grilled fish tacos, but all winter long we use the slow cooker to assist us in getting carne asada, carnitas, and shredded chicken to the table. Just like the pizza party in 3R, we put the rest of our fixings in small bowls and everyone makes their own taco(s) to their liking. Our favorite toppings are: pineapple slaw (page 105); mango salsa; pico de gallo; guacamole; black beans; hot sauce; sour cream; shredded cheese; and a squeeze of lime. Not every taco gets every topping, but at least it's all out there on the table. I cut corners and only make the coleslaw and the guacamole (Ina Garten's recipe) myself.

It might seem strange to pair an Old World influenced wine with tacos, but these wines love acid of all kinds and braised meat, so, the pairing actually works wonderfully. Just make sure your tacos are hefty. (A fish taco is not going to pair as well as one made with slow-cooked meat.) And 7R wines will pair just as well with a burrito from a local take-out joint!

PERFECT
PAIRINGS

Red meat

....

Stews

....

Mediterranean flavors

....

Herbs

....

Indian spices

....

High acid foods

FOODS TO
AVOID

Summer salads

ONE TO TRY

CHÂTEAU DE PIBARNON BANDOL (BANDOL, FRANCE)

SOME WINE STORIES ARE ABOUT THE people making the wine, but others are almost solely about the grape and the place. Of course, we want to honor the story of how Catherine and Henri de Saint Victor purchased the land that would become Château de Pibarnon in 1975 and turned it into the world-renowned vineyard that it is today. But the *real* story from Pibarnon is about the finicky and hard-to-grow Mourvèdre grape, and how it found a home in a terraced amphitheater overlooking the Mediterranean Ocean.

While the winemaking region of Provence has, in recent years, become popular for its rosé, the appellation of Bandol is best known for its stunning red wines, which are made from the Mourvèdre grape. Mourvèdre loves hot days but dislikes having dry roots, which can make it challenging to grow. It's also prone to mildew on its leaves. So, while the end result is a delicious wine, there are many regions throughout the world that simply can't grow it. Catherine and Henri realized that Château di Pibarnon could fulfill all of Mourvèdre's finicky requirements, and set out to capitalize on the property's unique qualities.

Château de Pibarnon is located in a tiny, hard-to-reach commune in Bandol, an area influenced by the strong Mistral winds that blow off of the Mediterranean and cool most of Southern France's winemaking regions. Pibarnon is unique because of its visually stunning, and yet incredibly practical, terraced amphitheater of vines. Sitting at the highest point in Bandol, the vineyards overlook the ocean, and would be buffeted day and night by the Mistral winds if not for the protection afforded them by the amphitheater. Instead, the warm, sunny days and long growing season give the slow-ripening Mourvèdre as much time as it needs to fully develop. The amphitheater,

meanwhile, lets in just enough wind to keep the leaves dry and free of mildew. The wind also imparts aromas from Provence's distinctive *garrigue*, or its low-growing vegetation and herbs, into the grapes— the essence of these famous Provençal herbs is unmistakably present in all of the region's wines.

Pibarnon is also lucky to have the most unique soil stratification in the entire appellation, with a top layer of stony Trias soil laden with fossils set over a forgiving base of blue clay. The top layer stresses the plants, while the clay retains enough moisture to keep them irrigated throughout the growing season.

With its polished earthiness and unique sense of place, Pibarnon has long been considered the best red wine in Bandol. It pairs beautifully with herbaceous, sweet yet savory meals that pull out the wine's inherent baking spices, dark red and black fruit, and licorice notes.

LET'S PAIR IT
Red Wine Duck with Green Olives and Dates over Polenta

Everyone needs a crowd-pleasing wine and food pairing in their back pocket that will wow a dinner party each time it hits the table. **The pairing of the Pibarnon Bandol with the following Red Wine Duck with Green Olives dish will ensure rave reviews, and second helpings all around.** The duck dish is very hearty and rich, but the Pibarnon cuts right through the sumptuousness while highlighting the brininess of the olives and the sweet fruit flavors of the sauce. This is a look-fancy-without-doing-too-much-work kind of dinner party dish, and the Bandol is universally adored, so feel confident to pair this meal and wine to any palate.

RED WINE DUCK
with GREEN OLIVES AND DATES OVER POLENTA

This is a great dinner party dish, as it can essentially all be done beforehand—even days ahead. Another classic play on sweet and salty, this recipe honors both the duck and the red wine, allowing them to provide an earthy, unctuous note while the dates and olives flit above and below. Good, pitted Castlevetrano olives or their brethren (Lucques, or others) are a near-must for this one. —GABRIEL

SERVES 4

8 duck legs
1 tablespoon canola oil
8 cloves garlic
24 pitted green olives
8 prunes, cut in half
8 dates, cut in half
8 shallots, peeled and cut in half
4 cups chicken stock
2 cups red wine
6 sprigs rosemary
4 sprigs thyme
Peel from 1 orange
Kosher salt and cracked black pepper

POLENTA
1½ cups milk
1½ cups chicken stock
1 cup polenta
¼ cup mascarpone
¼ cup butter
¼ cup grated Parmesan
Salt and pepper
1 tablespoon lemon juice
1 cup hot water

The night before, season the duck legs generously with kosher salt and black pepper. Refrigerate overnight.

Preheat oven to 275°F. Place a large sauté pan over high heat, and once hot, add the canola oil and the duck legs, skin side down. Sear until golden brown, about 6 to 7 minutes. Remove legs and set aside.

In an ovenproof casserole dish or Dutch oven, spread the garlic, olives, prunes, and dates over the bottom. Add the shallots and the duck legs, skin-side down.

In a saucepan, bring the stock, red wine, rosemary, thyme, and orange peel to a boil. Pour the mixture over the duck legs, without covering the legs completely. (The skin should still be visible.) Cover and place in the oven. Cook for 2 to 2½ hours, or until the duck legs begin to feel tender. Remove the casserole from the oven and carefully remove the duck legs, placing them skin-side up on a sheet pan.

Raise the oven temperature up to 400°F and place the sheet pan with the duck legs in the oven. Cook for 5 minutes until the skin is brown and crispy. Remove them from the oven and set aside.

Meanwhile, strain the liquid from the casserole dish; discard the orange peel and herb sprigs but reserve the remaining solids and the liquid. Skim as much fat as possible off the top of the liquid, then pour the liquid into a medium saucepot over medium-high heat and simmer until the liquid begins to reduce and thicken. Add the solids back to the liquid and remove from heat. To serve, place the duck legs over the polenta and liberally pour the sauce over the legs, making sure that the prunes, dates, olives, and shallots are well distributed.

POLENTA

In a medium saucepan, bring the milk and chicken stock to a boil. Slowly stir in the polenta. Reduce the heat to low, and cook until mixture is quite thick, about 30 minutes, stirring frequently. (Watch for scorching on the bottom of the pan.) Stir in the mascarpone, butter, and Parmesan, and season with salt and pepper to taste. If the mixture is too thick, add the hot water, 1 to 2 tablespoons at a time until the polenta reaches your desired consistency. Stir in the lemon juice.

THE CASHMERE SWEATERS OF THE WINE WORLD

MUCH LIKE THE WAY THE 7R WINES WE just learned about were basically beefed-up versions of 3R wines, the 8R wines are reminiscent of the lighter-bodied, yummy 4R wines. But instead of being, like, "Wow, this is yummy," it's now full-on caps lock, yelling in the comments section "THIS IS YUMMY!" Whenever TJ describes 8R wines he gets totally lost for words, ultimately looking at the customer and saying, "Listen,

AT A GLANCE

climate	Warm, sunny, and dry climates with long growing seasons
regions	Priorat and Toro, Spain; Napa Valley and Sonoma County, California; McClaren Vale, Australia; Swartland, South Africa; Languedoc-Roussillon, France; Puglia, Italy
varietals	Tempranillo, Cabernet Sauvignon, Zinfandel, Syrah/Shiraz, Grenache, Mourvèdre, Carignan, Negroamaro
technique	Riper grapes; longer maceration; longer periods of aging, primarily in new-oak barrels
characteristics	Abundant juice; overall smoother tannins with less acidity
color	Opaque burgundy, with garnet and purple tones
ideal pairings	A wide variety of meat and potato dishes including steaks, lamb, meatloaf, and burgers; Asian flavors; chicken thighs; Brassica vegetables such as brussels sprouts, broccoli, and kale

it just tastes GOOD." We also describe drinking these wines as being wrapped up in the perfect cashmere sweater.

While you'll absolutely find Merlot and Syrah in this section, West Coast Cabernet Sauvignon is king. 8R is the apex of ripe grapes, flavorful juice, long maceration, chewy tannic structure, and new wood aging. With some exceptions, that we'll get into in a moment, the wines here are New World in style with an emphasis on tasting good and making your mouth very, very happy. The American red wine palate is in love with 8R, because unlike European drinkers, we like to be able to drink wine without food. You can do that with these wines.

With warmer climates that encourage big, plump grapes, harvest times that push the envelope, and new wood aging that can last years, the winemakers have to constantly adjust their wines to maintain balance. Without careful control, these wines can feel overblown or sloppy, and are often pejoratively referred to as "fruit bombs." That means that they're all fruit and wood, with no acid or structure to rein everything in. We've seen a lot of winemakers in this book who believe in letting wine "do its thing," but up here, vigilance is needed.

One of the enduring fights of the wine world is whether or not these decadent wines deserve any respect. Many Europeans, and those with an Old World palate, will often say that they do not deserve respect because the purpose of wine is to enhance an experience with food, and that these wines lack the necessary balance to do that. But in our job we've seen *many* a dedicated Old World drinker accept these wines and appreciate them for what they are: well-made wines that taste like a dream.

GEEKOUT:
AMARONE, ITALY'S BIG BOY

There is an interesting Old World outlier in 8R: Italy's Amarone wines from the Valpolicella region in the Veneto. All techniques for making this wine are focused on one result: extracting as much flavor as possible from each grape. To that end, the indigenous grapes Corvina, Corvinone, and Rondinella (primarily) are grown in poor soil, so that the grape clusters are small and dense. Picked ripe, these grapes are left to dry for an average of 120 days. Traditionally, the grapes were left to dry on straw mats, but most wineries now dry them in dehydrators.

The juice inside the grape concentrates, and the tannins and color of the skin intensify as it shrivels. After this process, the grapes undergo an extra long maceration, which, again, extracts as much flavor and color from the grape as possible. The wines are then left to oak age for years, imparting additional nuances to the juice. These calculated techniques produce wines with huge taste and structure, and high alcohol. Even upon release, these wines are rarely ready to drink, but when left to age, soften, and mellow, they become more balanced and approachable without losing their full body. Amarone is the fullest-bodied wine that Italy makes.

All this effort costs the wineries dearly, and as a result Amarone is not always the most affordable wine on the market. But they're worth experiencing at some point in your wine journey as an example of how purposeful winemaker techniques can influence the finished product.

Our Favorite Regions and Varietals

Welcome to the New World. This is where the cowboys live. Our favorite regions for 8R are the ones that are doing something a little different, throwing the rules out the window, and making their wines the way they want to. There are more than a few rogues in this section, and their hope is that you drink their wines and have fun doing it.

SOUTH AFRICA

REGION: Swartland
VARIETAL: Cabernet Sauvignon, Grenache, Shiraz, Mourvèdre, Pinotage

As apartheid began to crumble in South Africa, winemakers began to revive vineyards that had been abandoned and left to fend for themselves. In many regions, these old vineyards were replaced with new vines. But in the region of Swartland, a movement was started to preserve the old bush vines and make interesting, unique wines from them. Gnarled vines, unique soils, and a devil-may-care attitude make Cabernet Sauvignon blends from this area unlike anything you've ever tasted. The winemakers aren't afraid to try new takes on the traditional Bordeaux and Rhône blends, and the resulting wines are full-bodied and New World in style. The Swartland winemakers are having fun reviving their vineyards and their region, and the wines show this carefree attitude.

SPAIN

REGION: Priorat
VARIETAL: Cariñena, Garnacha

Europe's long winemaking history makes it hard to discover a new region; however, colonizing winemakers have been reviving regions that were destroyed by natural or manmade disasters, or that fell out of favor over time. Such was the case with Priorat, which was ravaged by Phylloxera in the early 1900s and didn't recover until winemaker Rene Barbier revived the area in 1979. He was joined by four other wine renegades, and Priorat was reborn. Priorat grows Garnacha (Grenache), as well as Cariñena (Carignan), Syrah, Cabernet Sauvignon, and Merlot. It's hard farming on terrible soil up mountainous slopes, and winemakers aren't afraid to blend varietals to create a good wine. Priorat wines can be expensive. If they fall out of your price range, try the similarly styled valley wines of Montsant.

UNITED STATES

REGION: Napa Valley, California
VARIETAL: Cabernet Sauvignon

We're obsessed with the wines of Pritchard Hill in Napa, California, and it's not even an official AVA. It's more like a collection of mailboxes for some of the most famous winemakers in Napa. What it is, is sunny. And high up. And rocky. Finding any soil can sometimes be a challenge on Pritchard Hill. So why in the world are the likes of the Colgin, Chappellet, and Mondavi families farming there? Because the Cabernet Sauvignon grown up there in the full sun and terrible soil is some of the best we've ever tasted: powerfully and richly fruited with forceful but velvety soft tannins. By choice, Pritchard Hill may never be an AVA, but they fit nicely with this group of wine renegades.

WHAT TO EAT WITH
— 8R WINES —

While Europe's influence isn't totally gone by the time we've gotten this far up the Progressive Scale, the wines in this section are decidedly New World in body, taste, and attitude. They are also universally food-friendly, the only caveat being that you should not pair them with delicate foods that they will overwhelm. They're also drinkable on their own, so pour a glass while you're making dinner.

MEAT AND POTATOES

1 onion, diced

2 pounds ground beef

¾ cup breadcrumbs

¾ cup ketchup

Several dashes of Worcestershire sauce

2 tablespoons Dijon mustard

2 eggs

½ cup grated Parmesan

½ cup parsley

¼ cup basil

Salt and pepper

¼ cup water (optional)

One of the best pairings for this group of wines are meals made with ground beef. Yay, hamburgers! A thick, juicy burger with all the fixings is a match made in heaven with these thick, juicy wines. Ground beef is also a savior protein for busy working families with active kids.

Sometimes I try to class up my ground beef, and when I do that I make meatloaf, rosemary roasted potatoes, and steamed broccoli with olive oil and salt. I prefer throwing a bunch of stuff in a bowl and almost never measure, but here is a recipe for meatloaf to get you going.

Sauté the onion in oil or butter until soft. Place in a large bowl, then add all the additional ingredients, except for the water. Mix with your hands. Only add the water if it seems dry. Shape into a loaf in a roasting pan, coat with ketchup, and bake at 375°F for 1 hour and 15 minutes, or until it's cooked through.

PERFECT PAIRINGS

Burgers

Steaks

Meatloaf

Lamb

Chicken thighs

Cream and butter

Brussels sprouts and other Brassica family vegetables

Asian flavors

FOODS TO AVOID

Fresh fruit, fruit salsas, etc.

ONE TO TRY

LAIL VINEYARDS "BLUEPRINT" CABERNET SAUVIGNON (NAPA, CALIFORNIA)

AS A COUNTRY, AMERICA IS STARTING to add some rings around the tree, but the fact is, our winemaking traditions will never stretch as far back as Europe's. Compared to the winemaking of Ancient Greece or even the monks of Medieval Europe, America will always be the shiny new penny. But we aren't without impressive legacies of our own, and one of the best is currently represented by Robin Lail of Lail Vineyards.

Robin's legacy at Lail Vineyards originates with her great-granduncle, Gustave Niebaum (if you've ever been to Napa you're already perking up), who sailed into San Francisco with $600,000 of hard-earned seal pelts and eventually used that money to establish Inglenook Winery in Napa Valley in 1879. Yes, *the* Inglenook! Inglenook's wines were some of the first American wines to find international success, and won gold medals at the World's Fair of Paris in 1889. The estate was one of only ten Napa wineries to survive Prohibition, and Robin grew up playing in the vineyards around the famed Inglenook mansion on Highway 29.

Despite learning about wine from her grandfather and father, both of whom carried on the Inglenook tradition, Robin walked away from the wine business, and the family estate was sold in the 1960s. It was another Napa legend, Robert Mondavi, who lured Robin back into the industry by offering her a secretarial job. Before long, Robin was setting up her own successful vineyards, Dominus and Merryvale. Lail Vineyards was founded in 1995. It's the full realization of Robin's heritage and her deep connection to Napa Valley. Just like her great-granduncle, she's been making award-winning wines ever since.

Robin is an enchanting storyteller, and time spent with her never feels like long enough. Her wines carry the traditions of Napa, but are expressive and full of polish, much like Robin herself. Carefully planned, crafted, and executed, the wines offer a nod to history and an eye toward modernization with every sip. For most drinkers, the Lail wines are an investment, but they're worth your time, money, and interest. You cannot get through the first sip of the Blueprint Cabernet Sauvignon without closing your eyes and doing a little fist pump, thankful that the short history of wine that America *does* have includes Robin Lail.

LET'S PAIR IT
Lamb Chops Scottaditi

Lamb and Cabernet Sauvignon are known to taste great together, but we knew we needed a polished lamb dish to match the elegance of the Lail "Blueprint" Cabernet Sauvignon. **Luckily, Gabriel's Lamb Chops Scottaditi not only taste great with this Cali Cab, but they are also a match stylistically.** Much of the success of the pairing comes from the cohesion of the mint in the salsa verde with the menthol flavor in the wine. This grown up mint explosion stands in for the electric green mint jelly of our youth. The pairing won't make for a cheap date, but it will make for a memorable evening.

LAMB CHOPS SCOTTADITI

SERVES 4

LAMB CHOPS

8 lamb rib chops

Kosher salt and cracked black pepper

2 sprigs rosemary, leaves chopped

2 cloves garlic, chopped

1 tablespoon extra virgin olive oil

1 teaspoon brown sugar

Red pepper jelly

Salsa Verde (recipe below)

SALSA VERDE

1 shallot, diced fine

1 clove garlic, diced fine

4 tablespoons white wine vinegar

Zest of 1 lemon

2 tablespoons capers, rinsed and finely chopped

10 small anchovy filets, finely chopped

½ cup extra virgin olive oil

½ cup parsley, finely chopped

½ cup mint, finely chopped

Kosher salt

Some people like to trim the fat from their lamb chops—I prefer to leave it, thank you. If you prefer, you can also grill the chops for a nice char. Should you be the kind of person who finds themself with a jar of freshly made red pepper jelly (and you should; your mother would be so proud), save it for this use. Otherwise, a store-bought version will work just as well. —GABRIEL

Season the lamb chops with salt and black pepper. In a small bowl, combine the rosemary, garlic, olive oil, and brown sugar. Coat the chops with the mixture and refrigerate for 30 minutes. Place a large sauté pan over high heat until very hot. Cook the chops for 1½ to 2 minutes per side until the chops reach an internal temperature of 125°F. Let chops rest for 4 minutes; serve with red pepper jelly and Salsa Verde

SALSA VERDE

In a small mixing bowl, combine the shallot and garlic and cover with the vinegar. Add all of the other ingredients, except for the herbs, and stir to combine. Right before serving, stir in the herbs and season with salt to taste.

WINE GEAR

TJ loves wine gear. Drawers of corkscrews, cabinets of glassware, rows of decanters . . . we've got it all. As much as I might roll my eyes when he comes through the door with more gear, there are some necessary items that make drinking wine a more pleasurable experience. We've listed them here, in (our) order of importance.

Corkscrews

Unless you always buy screw-cap bottles, you're going to be out of luck if you don't have a corkscrew. We recommend a high-quality double-hinge corkscrew for most bottles. The double hinge is vital for ease of opening because it allows you to get leverage at two separate stages while easing out the cork. The Ah-So (or two-armed) wine pull is helpful for opening old bottles with crumbly or broken corks, but it's not our go-to opener. Once you learn to use the double hinge, you'll never go back. Skip the more expensive electric openers, and save your money for the wine.

Glassware

Your wine is open! Now where to put it? We do believe in varietal specific glassware, but we don't believe you need to go crazy about it. If you can, invest in thin crystal glassware like Riedel. If you can't, try to at least have a variety of differently shaped glasses that will handle whatever wine you buy. We recommend a Sauvignon Blanc glass for most white wines; a Burgundy glass for Pinot Noir and Chardonnay; a Bordeaux glass for Cabernet Sauvignon and other Bordeaux varietals; and Champagne flutes. (We prefer Champagne glasses with a slightly wider bowl than a traditional flute.) And always have ample stem-less options around for parties or for when you just don't care. We love the ones from Ikea. Along with your glassware, invest in a couple microfiber polishing rags to shine the glasses before pouring wine into them.

Decanters

If you're going to explore the world of full-bodied or aged red wines, you really need a decanter. It doesn't need to be expensive, and in a pinch we've even used a blender jar. Decanters come in all shapes and sizes, but we recommend ones with an indentation at the base so you can use your thumb to control the pour. We also recommend that the decanter has a flat top at the neck, so you can dry it upside down after cleaning. Glassware and decanters should always be hand-washed and dried upside down, on a rack if possible, to help with spotting.

Coravin

We are die-hard believers in the Coravin, a nifty contraption that allows you to access your wine without ever taking out the cork. It sounds too good to be true, but it's not! Using a hollow needle and compressed argon gas, the Coravin allows you to pour out sips or glasses of your wine, without letting any oxygen enter the bottle. The rest of the bottle can go back in your wine cellar or fridge, to drink another day. While the system is an investment, it immediately helps you save money by reducing those half-drunk bottles. It also lets you check in on your wine while it's aging. A revolutionary gadget!

The Best of the Rest

Thought not quite as critical as those listed above, it's worth adding a few incidentals to your arsenal.

Foil Cutters: We use the knife on our corkscrew, but many people swear by the ease of a foil cutter to help strip away the foil or wax found on the neck of corked bottles.

Non-Drip Pours: These are really helpful for gatherings, especially dinner parties when you don't want to drip on your guests' shoulders while pouring their wine. These inexpensive, thin disks go into the neck of the bottle and have saved many a tablecloth.

Chilling Pour Spouts: There's nothing worse than wanting a glass of white wine and not having a chilled bottle. Chilling pour spouts are great options for desperate moments.

An Aerator: We don't always have the time or desire to decant, and running the wine through an aerator as you pour it into your glass is a fantastic way to help you add oxygen to wine.

The One Thing You Don't Need

We think Champagne stoppers are the least important wine gadget. Sparkling wine is never as sparkly on Day Two, even with the stopper. So, we say: Just put in the extra effort to drink the whole bottle!

CHAPTER 9

THE LUSTY FRUIT BOMBS

We don't want to give away the end of the book, but there's not a whole lot of regional or varietal variation between the wines in this last chapter. They're big, they're bold, and they're beautiful unless, that is, you dislike full-bodied wines. But if you, like us, think there is a time and a place for every wine, then you, too, will embrace full-bodied wines as part of your overall portfolio. In the grand tradition of reclaiming pejorative names, we embrace the term lusty fruit bomb, and think we'll go right ahead and pour ourselves a glass!

9R

IT'S GETTING HOT, HOT, HOT!

WE'VE LEARNED ABOUT COLD-CLIMATE wines; we've visited continental climates; now all that is left to do is to dive into the warmest wine-producing regions in the world. 9R is all about sunshiny days, endless summers, and arid soils. For an added challenge, most regions require dry-farming, and even if they don't, winemakers typically shun regular irrigation. This stress helps the grapes maintain their all-important acidity.

AT A GLANCE

climate	Warm to hot climates with arid conditions; mostly New World
regions	Napa Valley and Dry Creek Valley, California; Walla Walla, Washington; Barossa Valley, Australia; Campania and Veneto, Italy; Mendoza, Argentina
varietals	Cabernet Sauvignon, Petite Sirah, Zinfandel, Syrah/Shiraz; Aglianico; Corvina; Malbec
technique	Harvest timed for optimal ripeness while maintaining acidity; long maceration; barrel fermentation and extended new-oak aging
characteristics	Full-bodied wines that are juicy, jammy, and richly tannic
color	Opaque with rich tones of burgundy, plum, and black
ideal pairings	Juicy, thick steaks and other red meat; barbecue; rich marinades; Osso Bucco; cream-based dishes; spicy foods

The thin-skinned grapes that we learned about at the start of the Progressive Scale are too delicate to grow in these hotter climates. The grapes here need thicker skins to protect them from drying out as they ripen. Vineyard maintenance, always an important aspect of winemaking, becomes even more vital in this section because the grapes are dependant on the shade from a leafy canopy—but too much greenery can sap vital resources from the grapes. Vineyard managers also prune the grape bunches judiciously, making sure that the strongest and best-placed clusters don't have to fight with less viable grapes for nutrients.

Because the growing conditions are hot and dry, the grapes are bursting with sugar at harvest time. Therefore, the full-bodied wines at this end of the scale tend to have very high alcohol levels, usually 15 percent or higher. Decanting or aerating the wines as you pour them helps some of this alcohol to escape, and helps the wine bring itself into balance before your first sip.

Oak aging, usually in new oak barrels, is also incredibly important, not only to help incorporate the alcohol into the wine, but also to help soften the tannins. These thick-skinned, darkly colored grapes have lots of tannin in them, and the tannins become part of the wine during maceration and fermentation. While a nice amount of gripping texture is pleasant in a wine, winemakers don't want you to feel like you're sucking on sandpaper when you take a sip. It can take years of aging to incorporate all of these elements into a drinkable wine.

9W wines are sometimes called a meal on their own, but they're also surprisingly food friendly in any season. You won't chug this wine, but from winter stews to summer barbecue, they are perfect to sip and savor.

GEEKOUT: **GLOBAL WARMING**

There is a rising sense of panic among vintners that global warming is slowly changing winemaking as they know it. Some times it works in their favor: For example, potential vineyard sites that historically have not gotten enough warmth now do, and this has expanded acreage sites for some. Other regions have been gifted a stretch of excellent vintages thanks to warm and dry weather. In other cases, vineyard managers have been able to successfully mitigate the effects of climate change by planting different varietals or changing the way they trellis the grapes.

But on the flip side, other areas, especially the warmers ones that we see in these later chapters, are expressing concern that their regions might not support grape growing in the coming decades. It's simply getting too hot. For others, the problem isn't too much heat—it's not enough. As temperature patterns change, some regions, like Burgundy, have had one spring after another in which their bud break has been damaged by hail, rain, and freezing temperatures. The basement cellars in Burgundy are only half filled, and that's a problem for their long-term viability. These days you cannot visit a winery anywhere without hearing a mention of climate change. Their hope is that they, and the grapes, can adapt over time to save their industry.

Our Favorite Regions and Varietals

There aren't a lot of regions on earth that grow these full-bodied, stain-your-teeth-purple, kind of wines. But for those of us who appreciate them, there are a lot of quality producers who know that making such a big wine that can also maintain balance is a challenge, and they take their mission seriously. Try to avoid high-volume producers, as they often use chemical shortcuts to make their wine taste more integrated.

AUSTRALIA

REGION: Barossa Valley
VARIETAL: Shiraz

Australian wines have gotten such a bad reputation over the last decade, and while wines like Yellowtail still dominate the wine market, we'd rather talk about some good Australian wine. Located in Southern Australia, Barossa Valley is a wine region that is now basking in acclaim thanks to the resurgence of Shiraz. Whether blended into a tasty GSM wine, or left to shine on its own, Shiraz from this region is chock-full of body, ripe black fruit flavors, cocoa, and spice. Barossa Valley supports both small boutique wineries and larger, more established producers like Penfolds. So, don't question Australia—embrace it!

UNITED STATES

REGION: Sonoma County, California
VARIETAL: Zinfandel

Dry Creek Valley, one of the most Northern AVAs in Sonoma and a neighbor of Alexander Valley, plants a few different varietals, but it's primarily known for one thing: Zinfandel. Dry Creek prides itself on being a bit of a backwater town, and the same can be said for its Zinfandel. Despite lacking an elegant polish,

the best Zinfandel in California, according to many people, comes from this 16-mile stretch of vineyards. The vineyards in Dry Creek benefit from an almost endlessly long and warm growing season, and also from the presence of old vines. These cranky old plants are not abundant fruit producers, but what they do grow is concentrated and full of flavor, made even more so by the area's microclimate.

ARGENTINA

REGION: Mendoza
VARIETAL: Malbec

Ok, hear us out with this one: It is true that most Malbec is not as full-bodied as a 9R, landing more often in 7R and 8R. However, as Argentina works hard to grow its incredible export business, their wines have become more full-bodied to appeal to the American palate. Additionally, the Malbec vineyards in regions like Mendoza are planted at incredibly high elevations and have the most consistent sun exposure of any grapes in the world, and we know that lots of sun equals bigger, more full-bodied wine. Blending with Cabernet Sauvignon and Syrah also helps to boost their heft. Fruity, spicy, minty, and yes, increasingly full-bodied, these modern style Argentinean wines have earned their place at the top of the scale.

WHAT TO EAT WITH
— 9R WINES —

If you head into any steakhouse in America, you're going to find a lot of 9R wines on the wine list. Their ubiquity could seem like laziness on the part of the wine directors, but the reality is that these wines need something big and flavorful to pair with—and steakhouses need wines that can stand up to slabs of red meat and creamed spinach. 9Rs do that, and do it beautifully.

ITALIAN COUNTRYSIDE SUPPER

Bone-in ribeyes
Salt and pepper
Arugula
Parmesan
Balsamic vinegar
Olive oil

One night in Umbria, Italy, we were lucky enough to have a multi-course meal prepared for us by a local chef. For our main course he made a meal that we are still trying to replicate—we've got the meal down, but we can't seem to reproduce the Italian view. With so much char, fat, and flavor, this dish stands up to the big body of 9R wines.

Light charcoal briquettes in a grill and let the flames die down to hot coals. Meanwhile, aggressively salt and pepper the steaks on both sides. When the coals have become hot embers, place the steaks directly into the embers. Cook on each side for approximately 3 minutes—you want a great sear on either side, but want them to stay medium rare. Remove to a cutting board and let sit for 10 minutes. Meanwhile, prepare a platter by spreading out the arugula. Slice the meat and arrange over top of the arugula. Drizzle the slices with the balsamic vinegar and olive oil, and add additional salt and pepper to taste. Top with freshly shaved Parmesan and serve immediately with many bottles of open, decanted wine.

PERFECT PAIRINGS

Red meat

Barbecue

Rich marinades

Osso bucco

Herbs

Cream

Spicy foods

FOODS TO AVOID

Citrus flavors

ONE TO TRY

BODEGAS ATECA "ATTECA OLD VINES" GARNACHA (CALATAYUD, SPAIN)

WE HAVE A PHRASE AT THE URBAN GRAPE that we believe in wholeheartedly: "cheap and cheerful." No matter where you are on your wine journey, and no matter how much you might be willing to pay for a bottle of wine, everyone needs some cheap and cheerful options in their arsenal. Ever since the day we opened The Urban Grape, one of our most endearingly popular wines has been the affordably priced Atteca Old Vines Garnacha from Bodegas Ateca in Spain.

Bodegas Ateca is owned by Gil Family Estates, a company founded four generations ago when Juan Gil began a small family winery in Jumilla, Spain. Their operations now include eight wineries all across Spain, with a dedication to producing wines made with each region's indigenous grapes. The company's other commitment is to keeping their wine prices low, a promise they can keep because of their wide array of labels. Amongst all of their brands, Gil Family Estates has wine that appeals to all palates—and this has made them one of the most popular wine producers in Spain.

The Atteca Garnacha is made from old Grenache vines that stretch up the slopes of the Ateca Mountains in the Calatayud region. Some of these vines are 100 years old, and they produce incredibly high-quality mountain fruit for the label. The juice is naturally big and bold, but somehow not overwhelming. Unlike other full-bodied wines that might spend years in oak, the Atteca only sees about 10 months of oak aging. Start to finish, the production of this wine is pretty quick, especially given its massive structure. That quick turn-around time helps the producers keep their costs down; they then pass that savings on to their customers.

The Atteca Garnacha is one of the most "corporate" wines that we've profiled in this book, and while some people might dismiss this wine because it's not unique enough, we do not. On the way home from work, after a long day, with more responsibilities looming between you and bed, sometimes you just want a glass of wine that tastes great, never lets you down, and goes with everything. This wine will pair with a quick steak salad, last night's take-out, or a bowl of popcorn. Or, you can dress it up and serve it at a dinner party and no one will raise an eyebrow. We all have a right to great tasting, cheap and cheerful wine. Never let the wine snobs tell you otherwise!

LET'S PAIR IT
Kabocha Squash and Sesame Rice Bowl

The wines in this chapter pair incredibly well with meat, and the Bodegas Ateca Garnacha is no exception. **But as this recipe for a Kabocha Squash and Sesame Rice Bowl shows, this Spanish wine pairs exceptionally well with sumptuous vegetarian dishes too!** The wine is masculine, with dark, red fruit and campfire smokiness. These flavors pair nicely with the sweetness of the squash and sweet potato, and the roasted flavor of the additional vegetables. The combination of the mushrooms with the soy vinaigrette brings umami earthiness to the pairing as well. The flavor combination with the wine is so convincingly meaty you'll swear there is steak in your rice bowl!

KABOCHA SQUASH
and SESAME RICE BOWL

SERVES 4

I call for kabocha here but if you can't find one, try butternut. Each of these components can be roasted at the same time and then combined in a bowl at the end. And while rice works great here, other grains, such as farro or quinoa can be substituted. —GABRIEL

1 small kabocha or butternut squash

Kosher salt and cracked black pepper

6 tablespoons extra virgin olive oil, divided

1 cup cooked brown rice

1 sweet potato, cut into 1-inch dice

4 king oyster mushrooms, cut into quarters

1 zucchini, sliced lengthwise, ¼-inch thick

1 clove garlic

Juice of 1 lemon

1 pinch red pepper flakes

1 ripe avocado

1 cup cooked brown rice

2 scallions, sliced thin on the bias

1 tablespoon mint leaves

1 tablespoon parsley leaves

Soy-Sesame Vinaigrette (recipe below)

¼ cup roasted whole almonds, roughly chopped

1 tablespoon toasted sesame seeds

SOY-SESAME VINAIGRETTE

¼ cup dark soy sauce

3-4 tablespoons maple syrup

¼ cup sherry vinegar

Zest of 1 orange

1 small piece ginger, peeled (about the size of a thumb)

1 small dried chile (chile de arbol would be perfect)

2 sprigs mint

2 sprigs lemon verbena

2 tablespoons sesame oil

Preheat oven to 400°F and place a baking sheet on the middle rack.

Cut the squash into quarters, remove the seeds, and season the flesh with salt and pepper. Pour 2 tablespoons of olive oil over the flesh, and place quarters on the pre-heated baking sheet. Cook for 45 minutes, or until tender.

Meanwhile, toss the sweet potato in a bowl with 1 tablespoon olive oil and season with salt and pepper. Pour sweet potato slices onto one half of a baking sheet. Toss the oyster mushrooms with 1 tablespoon olive oil and season with salt and pepper; place mushrooms on the other half of the baking sheet. Add the sweet potatoes and mushrooms to the oven and roast for about 15 to 20 minutes, or until well caramelized. (Mushrooms may cook more quickly; check after 10 minutes.) Remove and reserve. Lay the zucchini slices on a lightly oiled piece of parchment paper on a baking sheet. Using a Microplane, grate the garlic over the zucchini, then drizzle with 1 tablespoon lemon juice, and season with salt and red pepper flakes. Drizzle 1 tablespoon olive oil over the zucchini and roast in the oven until the zucchini starts to caramelize, about 8 minutes. Remove and reserve.

Once squash is tender, remove from the oven and scoop the flesh from the skin. Pass the squash through a food mill or a ricer, or mash with a fork, and set aside.

Dice the avocado and dress with 1 tablespoon olive oil, a squeeze of lemon juice, salt, and pepper.

To serve: Scoop some of the rice into each bowl and top with a small amount of each of the prepared vegetables. Garnish with scallion, parsley, and mint, and dress with 2 tablespoons or more of the Soy-Sesame Vinaigrette. Top with almonds and sesame seeds. Serve warm.

SOY-SESAME VINAIGRETTE

This recipe yields more vinaigrette than needed—but it can also be used as a marinade for the Grilled Short Ribs recipe (page 219). Note: If you can't find lemon verbena, just double the mint.

Combine soy sauce, 3 tablespoons maple syrup, sherry vinegar, orange zest, ginger, chile, mint, lemon, and lemon verbena in a medium saucepot over medium heat. Bring to a simmer and reduce liquid by half. Strain, and let cool to room temperature. Add sesame oil and stir to combine; taste and add up to 1 more tablespoon maple syrup if desired. Store in an airtight container in the refrigerator for 1 to 2 months.

VARIATIONS ON A THEME

THE RED WINES AT THIS END OF THE Progressive Scale—made almost exclusively from Zinfandel, Syrah (Shiraz), Petite Sirah, and Cabernet Sauvignon—are, in a word, massive. There can be no debate about their huge body, intense fruit, oak influence, or tannic structure. Like the foundation of a well-made house, these four influences on the wine have to be in perfect balance, or the wine's walls will start to crumble. Warm, New World regions dominate, with a rare exception for the most full-bodied Amarone wines.

climate	Primarily the hottest and most arid growing regions
regions	Walla Walla, Washington; Barossa Valley, Australia; Napa Valley and Paso Robles, California; Veneto, Italy
varietals	Syrah/Shiraz, Petite Sirah, Zinfandel, Corvina
technique	Very ripe fruit; new-oak fermentation and barrel aging; long periods of aging in barrel and bottle
characteristics	Massive wines that are dense and flavorful with a mouthfeel of heavy cream; thick and jammy
color	Opaque, rich burgundy, plum, and black colors
ideal pairings	Barbecue; balsamic reductions; richly flavored stews; umami flavors; rich, bold cheeses

We can't examine the wines of 9R and 10R without talking about the "Parkerization" of wine, a reference to the influence that wine critic Robert Parker has had over winemaking during the last several decades. As the modern era's most influential critic, his points system has the ability to change the fortune of wineries by motivating wine buyers to clamor for their highly rated products. Increased demand means increased prices and revenue, as well as the coveted name recognition that is hard for wineries to attain, but once achieved seems to last forever.

Although Parker often denies having a palate bias, the general consensus is that he seems to prefer highly extracted, high alcohol, highly oaked wines with a bombastic fruit finish. In an effort to score big points with him, wineries started shifting their winemaking techniques to produce these heaviest-bodied wines. The hope was to achieve a score in the high 90s, or even achieve the coveted 100-point rating. In our opinion, this doesn't make the wine bad, but can make the wines from different regions and producers seem very similar.

We are asked all the time if a 100-point wine is "worth it." Here is our answer: YOU are ultimately the wine critic. If a 100-point Parker wine tastes like a 100-point wine to you, then yes, his score should influence you. However, if these wines are unappealing to you, then no score is ever going to make you like them. Buy to your palate first and foremost. The only exception to this rule is if you are building a cellar that you hope to resell, because the Parker-approved wines do typically age and appreciate well. And, newer wine drinkers do gravitate to these wines, because their fruitier style and integrated tannins are less intimidating as you're learning about red wine. Do *we* like them? Yup, we do. They have a time and a place, and are often unabashedly delicious.

GEEKOUT: WHY SO EXPENSIVE?

A lot of the fullest-bodied wines, both red and white, are more expensive than their lighter-bodied peers. Customers always want to know: What gives? First and foremost, the issue is land. Many European producers are cultivating vineyards that were paid off generations ago, while new Napa producers have to buy land at up to $300,000 per acre! Other American regions are cheaper, but the land still needs to be purchased and vines planted before production can start. American producers are also expected to have state-of-the-art grounds, cellars, and tasting rooms. These expenses are reflected in the price.

Full-bodied wines also need longer oak aging, often in new oak barrels. Thus, oak barrels become a big yearly expense, and it takes years for the resulting wines to go to market and finally offset the cost of producing them. That's a lot of overhead. Even small expenses, like bottling the wine in thicker glass bottles, add up.

Lastly, because demand for these wines is at an all-time high, the producers can charge whatever the market will bear. And the market bears a lot. It can make these wines out of reach for most wine drinkers.

Our suggestions remain the same: Look for less popular vintages, up-and-coming regions, second or sister labels, and lesser-known producers to experience these wines at a fraction of the price.

Our Favorite Regions and Varietals

There aren't too many regions outside of the West Coast that make 10R wines, but even though our options have shrunk geographically, there is still a lot of variety between producers. Napa Valley has earned its status of King of the American Reds, but lesser known regions are worth exploring, too.

UNITED STATES

REGION: Napa Valley, California
VARIETAL: Cabernet Sauvignon

There's simply no place like Napa. There's money in those hills, but everyone is still walking around in their Wranglers and boots. People who love Napa wine first talk about whether the grapes are "valley floor" or "mountain fruit." The flats of Napa are planted with acre after acre of pristinely manicured vines. It's mesmerizing and perfect. Meanwhile, the mountain fruit is tucked on vineyards up and down the Vaca and Mayacamas mountain ranges, struggling for nutrients in the poor soils. The mountain fruit wines tend to be more intense and tannic, and are also better protected from standing water during rainy vintages. Napa has 16 official sub-regions, ranging from established areas like Howell Mountain to up-and-comers like Coombsville. We love them all.

UNITED STATES

REGION: Paso Robles, California
VARIETAL: Zinfandel

The official Paso Robles wine website says that the region's town feels like it's right out of a Norman Rockwell painting, but as we established in the white wine section, when Paso emerged it had a reputation for being the wild, wild West. In the years that have passed, Paso Robles has become more mainstream, but the energy and pioneering spirit still remain. While Napa is known for its Cabernet Sauvignon, Paso Robles has made its mark by producing undeniably yummy, full-bodied Zinfandel. Spicy and brambly with excellent fruit and enormous alcohol, these are the perfect wines for a steak cooked on an open flame, bringing out the cowboy in all of us.

UNITED STATES

REGION: Walla Walla, Washington
VARIETAL: Syrah

Walla Walla is one of our favorite American winemaking regions, and while it produces a lot of excellent Cabernet Sauvignon, we also love the full-bodied, inky Syrahs made in the northern-most parts of the region. These wines are so deeply purple that they almost look black. The Walla Walla Syrahs are meaty, both in body and in flavor, with earthy black olive and dense fruit flavors. Walla Walla sits in the Northeast corner of the state, and even bleeds into Oregon. Climatically, the region is known for extremes. The winters are cold, but the summers are long and hot, with very little rainfall. With all that sun and warmth, the grapes could get overly ripe, but cool nights help them to retain acidity that saves the final product.

WHAT TO EAT WITH
— 10R WINES —

10R wines are so massive, dense, and flavorful that you don't always need *to pair them with food to enjoy them—and sometimes, pairing them to the right meal can be overwhelming. But, there are foods that can stand up to their heft— and they're usually the most filling ones.*

HEARTY BEEF STEW

2 pounds beef stew meat

Salt and pepper

Flour

Oil

Onions (I use pearl onions)

Mushrooms, sliced

Squeeze of tomato paste

2 cups red wine

Several dashes of Worcestershire sauce

A variety of vegetables in big chunks (potatoes, carrots, turnips, parsnips, sweet potatoes, butternut squash— pick and choose what sounds good)

Beef broth

Thyme

Peas

Parsley

Grated Parmesan

Beef stew is a meal that I've made so many times that I don't even look at a recipe anymore, but if you need a starting point, Tyler Florence, Ina Garten, and Smitten Kitchen all have great recipes. Here's what we do:

Season the meat with the salt and pepper. Dredge the meat in flour. Heat oil in a straight-sided sauté pan, and sear the meat in several batches, being careful not to crowd the pieces. Reserve. Add the pearl onions and mushrooms and roll them around in the yummy stuff at the bottom of the pan. Add the tomato paste and Worcestershire sauce, and stir to combine. Slowly add in the red wine, scraping the bottom of the pan. Dump the meat and onion-mushroom-wine sauce into a slow cooker. Add all the vegetables, thyme, and enough beef broth to just cover everything. Give it a stir and set your slow cooker to low for 6 to 8 hours. If you can, stir it every two hours or so. About 30 minutes before serving, add the peas. Serve topped with chopped parsley and grated Parmesan.

PERFECT **PAIRINGS**

Richly flavored stews

Barbecue

Umami flavors

Rich, boldly flavored cheeses

Honey

Balsamic reductions

FOODS TO **AVOID**

Sushi

ONE TO TRY

LUCA "LABORDE DOUBLE SELECT" SYRAH (MENDOZA, ARGENTINA)

THERE ARE SO MANY STORIES TO TELL about the Luca Double Select Syrah that it's almost hard to know where to begin. The vines themselves have a unique history; it's a drink anywhere/any time kind of wine; it's an eternal bestseller at UG; and the entire operation is headed up by two, truly kick-ass women: owner Laura Catena (a doctor and mother in her spare time), and female winemaker Estela Perinetti. Let's hashtag this one #girlpower.

The story begins with viticulturist Luis Laborde, who traveled throughout the Rhône Valley to find the best Syrah rootstock in France. He brought the vines back to his hometown of Mendoza, where he planted them in a small research vineyard. There, he laboriously tracked each vine's adaptation to the Argentinian climate and soil, as well as the quality of the grapes. The best of the best were re-planted in a working vineyard, and it is these vines that produce the grapes for the Laborde Double Select—vines that were chosen for excellence not once, but twice.

Like Luis Laborde, Laura Catena's father, Nicolas, was a true wine pioneer in the emerging Argentinean wine scene of the 1980s and '90s, and passed his love of wine to his daughter. In addition to being an emergency room doctor in San Francisco, Laura now runs her family's winery, Bodega Catena Zapata, as well as oversees her own brand, Luca. She's one of the country's most passionate supporters of Argentinian wine, and has continued her father's legacy of expanding the breadth and reach of their exports into new wine markets.

Laura Catena and her head winemaker, Estela Perinetti, represent an ever-growing and influential part of the wine world: women. Old World traditions often precluded fathers from handing down their vineyards to their daughters, believing instead that it was a son's privilege to take over the family business. These days, daughters often succeed their fathers, and throughout the world, women are studying oenology and launching successful careers as winemakers. If you'll allow us to stereotype, we find that female winemakers have a gentler, more patient approach to winemaking, and that their wines are almost always balanced, nuanced, and intriguing. And while it's true that across the board these women want to be known as excellent winemakers (not excellent *women* winemakers), they are paving the way for future generations of women to have successful careers in wine.

The Luca Syrah has all of these qualities, and has been one of our best-selling wines for several years. No matter the season, there's always a perfect pairing for this outstanding, carefully crafted, and affordable wine.

LET'S PAIR IT
Grilled Boneless Short Ribs with Brussels Sprouts

The Luca Syrah is a classic Argentinian wine—peppery dark berry fruit with smoked meat overtones—so it's no surprise that it pairs so effortlessly with the following Grilled Boneless Shortribs and Brussels Sprouts recipe. The grilled smokiness of the short rib magnifies the meatiness of the wine, while the Syrah effortlessly handles the funkiness of the Brussels sprouts. But it's the chestnuts that steal the show by pulling out the toasty wood in the wine, creating a warming sensation that travels throughout the memorable pairing.

GRILLED BONELESS SHORT RIBS
with BRUSSELS SPROUTS

SERVES 4

Four 6-8 ounce portions of boneless short ribs

6 tablespoons Soy-Sesame Vinaigrette (see page 210), divided

2 ounces slab bacon, diced

1 pound Brussels sprouts, quartered

1 tablespoon butter

2 ounces roasted, jarred chestnuts, chopped

2 tablespoons picked parsley leaves, chopped

2 tablespoons mint leaves, chopped

Kosher salt and cracked black pepper

One possible title for this recipe was "OHMYGOD grilled boneless short ribs are so good." (This is completely true . . . in my mind, at least.) This dish puts that all-purpose Soy-Sesame Vinaigrette to good use (page 210). Also, if chestnuts are unavailable, hazelnuts or even salted peanuts would be a fine substitute. —GABRIEL

Coat short ribs in 2 tablespoons of the Soy-Sesame Vinaigrette and let marinate, refrigerated, for 30 minutes.

Preheat oven to 450°F and light a grill to high heat.

Put a cast iron sauté pan over high heat. Cook bacon until rendered. Using a slotted spoon, set bacon aside, reserving the fat in the pan. Add the Brussels sprouts to the pan. Season with salt and pepper and let cook undisturbed for 3 minutes. Stir in butter, then transfer the pan to the oven. Cook until sprouts are caramelized but still a little firm, 5 to 10 minutes. Remove pan from the oven and add the rendered bacon, chestnuts, and mint. Add remaining 4 tablespoons of vinaigrette to the pan and toss to combine.

Meanwhile, season the short ribs with salt and pepper and put them over a hot grill. Flip the short ribs every minute or so, and cook until they reach an internal temperature of 124°F for medium rare. Let rest 5 minutes before slicing them against the grain and serving them with the Brussels sprouts.

HOW TO ORDER WINE AT A RESTAURANT

Ordering wine in a restaurant is one of the single most intimidating wine experiences on earth, especially if you're ordering for the whole table. All eyes are on you as you peruse the wine list—a jumble of producers, varietals, and regions you've never heard of and certainly can't pronounce. You have to please a variety of palates, dishes, and spending habits. But seriously, no pressure. You can survive this, we promise. Here's how.

Do Your Research

For the first two years of our relationship, every time we went on a date, I would stare at TJ, who would be staring at the wine list, for 20 minutes. Now, he looks at the list online beforehand so he has a sense of the direction he wants to take. Perusing the list before you hit the restaurant is always a good idea so you can get your bearings. But you'll never fully get out of looking at the list while at the restaurant, so we make this part of the night more enjoyable by ordering a cocktail or glass of sparkling wine to enjoy during the process.

Ask for Help

Even sommeliers remember what it was like to get confused by the differences between Burgundy and Bordeaux. A huge part of their job is to act as your wine-buying guide. If the restaurant does not have a sommelier, ask your waiter. If your waiter does not know how to help you, ask for the manager. Even the most seasoned wine people ask for help with wine lists; there is no stigma in calling in the experts.

Know Your Budget

It is not only okay, it is absolutely expected that you will have a wine budget for your dinner. Please don't feel embarrassed to ask for recommendations in your price range. If discretion is needed, simply point to a bottle price that feels right to you and tell your waiter or sommelier that you're looking for something in a similar price range. They may also recommend wines in the next

bracket, but a good sommelier will always respect your budget. Unusual varietals or regions are a great place to find some value.

Find a Common Language

The more descriptive you can get in describing wines you like, the easier it will be for your waiter to help you pick the right bottle. Describe the weight of the wine you'd like (skim milk, whole milk, heavy cream), any flavors you prefer (red fruit, purple fruit, spicy like peppercorns versus spiced like nutmeg), and the textures you like or dislike. Some people really don't like heavy tannins, and that's ok! Whatever you do, push yourself to move beyond words like "dry" or "fruity" to words that really describe what you'd like. And remember, yummy is a great descriptor!

Play to the List's Strengths

Also known as: When in Rome, don't drink Australian. If you're at an Italian restaurant, order an Italian wine. In a French restaurant, go French, and so on. It's sure to effortlessly pair with the meal, no matter what you order, and the chances are good that the wine director has put more effort into choosing wines that fit the restaurant's theme.

Don't Forget, *Drink Progressively!*

And, of course, pair to your meal, whenever possible. This can be challenging when you're trying to please a whole table of people who are ordering a variety of entrees, but learning the basic pairing strategies laid out in this book will help you navigate any wine list.

START EXPLORING

THROUGHOUT THIS BOOK, TJ AND GABRIEL have shared their expertise in an attempt to help you demystify the expansive world of wine, and pairing wine to food.

Now, it's my turn to give you one final pep talk. Between TJ, Gabriel, and myself, I am the one who is most like you: an average wine drinker who struggles to make sense of the world of wine every single day. I have stood in a wine store—even my own—and felt rising panic as I tried to zero in on a bottle for dinner. I've even committed that cardinal sin: For years I did not know that Chablis meant Chardonnay.

That's why I know that this way of thinking about wine truly works. Once you have learned the fundamental aspects of the Progressive Scale, you can apply it in any wine store or restaurant, no matter how the selection is set up. Have confidence that after reading this book, you know when to drink the lightest bodied wines, and what to pair with them. You understand why meat and potatoes pair with the heaviest red wines—and if you ever forget, just check the cheat sheets throughout this book.

The building blocks of your wine knowledge are right here—now, you just need to practice. It's a cliché, but it's true—the end of this book is the beginning of your wine journey. All you have to do is get out there and start to *Drink Progressively!*

—Hadley

ABOUT THE AUTHORS

TJ AND HADLEY DOUGLAS
OWNERS, THE URBAN GRAPE

TJ and Hadley Douglas are the husband and wife owners of The Urban Grape, a ground-breaking and wildly popular wine store in Boston. The store concept is simple, but revolutionary: *Drink Progressively.* Their system of sorting wine by its body, instead of by varietal or region, brings ease and an unexpected surprise to customers, and business is booming as a result. The Urban Grape has won accolades as Boston's Best Wine store from both *Boston* magazine and *The Improper Bostonian*, as well as a 50 on Fire award from BostInno, an innovation think tank in the city.

As the wine buyer, head sales person, and architect of Progressive Shelving for The Urban Grape, TJ is directly responsible for the store's success. He has been profiled by *Boston* magazine, *Boston Common*, *The Boston Globe*, *The Boston Herald*, *The Improper Bostonian*, *Massachusetts Beverage Journal*, and Terroirist. Thanks to TJ's leadership, The Urban Grape was also called "Boston's Revolutionary Wine Store" in a cover story for *Beverage Dynamics*. He has taught classes on drinking progressively at the Boston Center for Adult Education, and at events like the Boston Wine Expo. TJ also consults with area restaurants on making their wine lists more user-friendly and accessible.

Hadley's background is in marketing, events, and philanthropic management. If TJ's job is to sell what's in the store, Hadley's is to sell the store itself. She has built a loyal community through Twitter, Facebook, and her widely read blog and weekly newsletters. Hadley coordinates wine-focused lifestyle content for websites like Style Me Pretty, Living, and Racked, and

in magazines like *Boston Home*. The official voice of The Urban Grape, Hadley translates "wine speak" to UG's customers in a clear, fun, and vibrant way. Additionally, she directs all of the store's charitable giving, ensuring that the store is a good community partner to its customers and to the South End neighborhood where the store is located.

Together, TJ and Hadley are the parents of two wonderful boys, Noah and Jason, who were each selling Pinot Noir on the playground by the age of three. When TJ and Hadley are not drinking and selling wine, they can be found hiking, skiing, and beaching it with their sons, and the family dog, Zeus.

GABRIEL FRASCA

EXECUTIVE CHEF/PARTNER, STRAIGHT WHARF RESTAURANT

Gabriel Frasca is the Boston-born, North Shore-raised, executive chef/partner at Nantucket's acclaimed Straight Wharf restaurant. A veteran of both Boston and New York restaurants, Frasca counts the likes of Michael Schlow, David Bouley, Paul O'Connell, and Seth Woods amongst his mentors. His restaurants have been recognized by publications and websites like *The New York Times*, *The Boston Globe*, *Food & Wine*, *Gourmet*, *Saveur*, Starchefs.com, and others, and have won awards, including *Boston* magazine's best restaurant nine times, as well as a Best New Chef nod for Frasca himself.

Frasca splits his time between Nantucket, where he works, and Sudbury, where he runs a small childcare non-profit with Amanda Lydon (their clients include only their two children, Marin and Henry). Frasca, who peaked sometime during his junior year of high school, specializes in pretending that he can help his kids with their math homework. He cannot. A board member of Sustainable Nantucket, and the owner of Nantucket's only Certified Green Restaurant, Frasca spends as much time outdoors as possible.

ACKNOWLEDGEMENTS

TJ AND HADLEY DOUGLAS

All wine journeys start with a moment or two of inspiration. Ours started with Cat Silirie and Kevin Zraly. Cat: Who knew that learning about wine with you in a living room so long ago would lead to all of this? Thank you for lighting the initial flames, and thank you, Mr. Zraly, for inspiring our entire concept.

To everyone at The Aquitaine Group and Ruby Wines, but particularly Jeff Gates and Brad Rubin, thank you for your unfailing support in the early years of TJ's exploration into wine.

To the Charlie's Angels trio of Danielle Chiotti, Erin Byers Murray, and Nicole Kanner – none of this could have happened without the three of you so solidly in our corner. Thank you for calming every fear and freak-out from inception to publication. Thank you, as well, to Matthew Teague and Paul McGahren of Spring House Press for taking in our project and overseeing it with such thoughtfulness.

Gabriel, from the day we called you with this idea you were in, all the way. And every day since you've been in, all the way. You're a magnificent chef, and because of you we now know how to poach an egg, fry a chicken thigh, and cook a perfect duck leg. Thank you for the encouraging texts, the homerun recipes, and the many meals we've shared along the way. Here's to many more collaborations.

Thank you to our many recipe testers and menu-tasting neighbors, and to Béatrice Peltre for your exceptional photography. You made our vision come to life, and our book is more beautiful for your efforts.

Thank you to Nancy Bean for opening your home to us on Nantucket, and to Brahm Callahan, MS, for lending us your incredible wine knowledge as a fact checker for the book. Chris Howell, we've admired you, your winemaking philosophy, and your wines for over 15 years. We cannot thank you enough for writing such a thoughtful foreword for *Drink Progressively*.

To the winemakers: You give a gift to the world with every bottle. Thank you for producing wine that is so fun to sell, for sharing your stories with us, and for your unfailing support of The Urban Grape.

Our store and book would not have been possible without the hard-working and energetic staff of The Urban Grape, past and present. Your passion is inspiring, your dedication to hospitality legendary. Our pride in you knows no bounds. A special thank you to our right-hand woman, Chelsea Bell, for reading every sentence, and helping us to fill in the holes when needed.

For our customers, it has always been about you. Thank you for your support, your loyalty, and your passionate exploration of wine. Choosing wine for you gives us endless joy, and we've found a home and extended family with you in the South End.

Thank you to our families for giving us the love of food, wine, and family dinner. And lastly, for Jason and Noah, about whom there will never be enough words to describe our love. Sitting around the dinner table with you each night is the greatest gift of our lives.

GABRIEL FRASCA

By the a time a plate hits the pass at Straight Wharf, it isn't the work of the one cook who finished it, but rather the product of a team that has seamlessly come together to make the whole much more than the sum of its parts. My contribution to this book should be described in much the same way.

Firstly, I must thank TJ and Hadley for letting me be a part of this project, and to Erin Byers Murray for patiently walking me though all of this. (At one point Erin told me I could write notes and send her pictures of said notes; if it is not too late, I would like to take her up on her offer). I need also to thank Mayumi Hattori and Andrea Solimeo, our chefs de cuisine, who lent me their knowledge, experience, and in some cases, their recipes. Sous chefs Greg Alessi, Miguel Hernandez, Lisa Chu, and Edinar Piano each rescued me at various stages of this process; without them, I'd still be trying to make the pork shanks look appetizing, scrubbing oysters for the shoot, or trying to measure the spices for the sausage.

Thanks always to Jock Gifford for being the Chairman of the Board. I am also extremely grateful to our sommeliers for tasting through the wines with me, particularly Tanya McDonough, ever-indulgent and kind, and Scott Fraley, who repeatedly did his rain man-thing where he would show up with a radish and a chunk of parm and, correctly, completely overrule any dish ideas we had up to that point.

So many of our neighbors chipped in to loan us the perfect plate, an amazing fork, or the linen that made the shot; so Atlantic, Nantucket Looms, Greydon House, Mike Lascola, and others, I am overwhelmed by your generosity, your hospitality, and your willingness to trust me with your beautiful things.

Finally, I owe my largest debt of gratitude to my inveterate tasters, Marin and Henry, and to my editor-in-chief, Amanda Lydon. Without them, none of this would have been possible; their patience, support, and inexhaustible supply of better ideas (looking at you, Hanker) make me less bad at this, and most other things, every single day. So, to them, and to every other cook, chef, mentor, or book that I've spent even a moment with, I offer my most sincere thanks, and this chilling statement: You've made me what I am today.

APPENDIX

THE WHITES

1W

Climate: The coolest alpine- and maritime-influenced regions of Europe

Regions: Txakoli, Spain; Minho, Portugal; Languedoc and Savoie,France; and Valle D'Aoste, Italy

Varietals: Hondarrabi Zuri; Alvarinho/Albariño; Picpoul de Pinet; Jacquère; Prié Blanc

Technique: Steel-fermented, no aging or oak influence

Characteristics: Remarkably light-bodied with a mouthfeel like skim milk; tart, lip-smacking acidity

Color: Straw-hued or pale green

Ideal Pairings: Oysters, shellfish, and white fish; ceviche; light dishes and salads that have bright acidity

2W

Climate: Cool alpine- and maritime-influenced regions

Regions: Finger Lakes, New York; Muscadet and Sancerre, France; Alto Adige, Italy

Varietals: Riesling, Melon de Bourgogne, Sauvignon Blanc, Pinot Grigio

Technique: Mostly stainless-steel fermented; but some sur lie aging

Characteristics: Light-bodied with a mouthfeel resembling skim milk; bright acidity

Color: Pale straw-hued

Ideal Pairings: Grilled shrimp and calamari; scallops ceviche; oysters; crab salad; cucumber, melon, green apple

3W

Climate: Slightly warmer and sunnier regions; primarily alpine- and maritime-influenced

Regions: Tuscany and Campania, Italy; Alsace, France; Willamette Valley, Oregon; Marlborough, New Zealand; Napa Valley, California

Varietals: Vernaccia, Falanghina, Riesling, Pinot Grigio/Gris, Sauvignon Blanc

Technique: Primarily steel fermented; some aging in concrete eggs or neutral-oak barrels; some sur lie

Characteristics: Between light and medium body with increased fruit and texture and a mouthfeel of 1% milk; vibrant acidity

Color: Pale yellow

Ideal Pairings: Sushi; spring vegetables; aromatic herbs; white meat and firm white fish; soft, mild cheeses

4W

Climate: A mix of warm and cool climates; some Mediterranean ocean influences

Regions: Alsace, Burgundy, and Loire Valley, France; Tuscany, Italy; Columbia Valley, Washington; Stajerska, Slovenia; Willamette Valley, Oregon; Niederösterreich, Austria

Varietals: Riesling, Chardonnay, Chenin Blanc, Vermentino, Semillon, Pinot Grigio/Gris, Grüner Veltliner

Technique: Some winemaker influence using sur lie aging, light skin contact, and/or neutral wood aging; no malolactic fermentation (ML)

Characteristics: Enhanced body, texture, and complexity with sweeter fruit nuances and a mouthfeel of 2% milk

Color: Yellow with golden hues

Ideal Pairings: Light pasta dishes; Mediterranean dishes; firm, fatty fish; grilled chicken sausages; spicy take-out food

5W

Climate: A mix of cool and warm regions

Regions: Napa Valley and Santa Barbara County, California; Bordeaux, Languedoc-Roussillon, and Burgundy, France; Mosel Valley, Germany; Le Marche, Italy

Varietals: Sauvignon Blanc, Semillon, Grenache Blanc, Marsanne, Chardonnay, Riesling, Verdicchio

Technique: A light-handed mix of techniques including residual sugar, partial malolactic fermentation, and minimal oak aging

Characteristics: Softer texture and smooth finish; enhanced fruit, refreshing acidity, and a mouthfeel of whole milk

Color: Yellow with golden tones

Ideal Pairings: Spicy-sweet foods; curry dishes; pasta or seafood with light butter/citrus sauces; roasted white meats; mushrooms and garlic

6W

Climate: Increased warmth and sunshine; some Mediterranean-style climates
Regions: Rhône Valley and Burgundy, France; Sicily, Italy; Goriska Brda, Slovenia; Mosel, Germany
Varietals: Grenache Blanc, Marsanne, Roussanne, Viognier, Chardonnay, Carricante, Catarratto, Ribolla Gialla, Riesling
Technique: A mix of winemaker techniques including partial malolactic fermentation and oak aging
Characteristics: Integrated acidity and minerality with a creamy texture and a mouthfeel of whole milk
Color: More golden-hued than yellow
Ideal Pairings: Creamy dishes with citrus notes; root vegetables; veal; oil, butter, and jus sauces; chilled fish salads

7W

Climate: Warmer Old and New World regions with abundant sunshine
Regions: Rioja, Spain; Santa Barbara County, San Luis Obispo County, and Sonoma, California; Burgundy, Alsace, and Loire Valley, France
Varietals: Viura, Chardonnay, Gewürztraminer, Chenin Blanc, Grenache Blanc, Marsanne, Roussanne, Viognier
Technique: Partial or full malolactic fermentation with a mix of new- and old-oak aging
Characteristics: Ripe fruit, softer texture, and fuller body with a mouthfeel like half-and-half; mineral-driven with acid present
Color: Bright, golden hues
Ideal Pairings: Game meats; earthy vegetables; firmer, lower acidity cheese; cream sauces over white meats and veal

8W

Climate: Warm climates with lots of sun and large temperature shifts from day to night (diurnal shift)
Regions: Mendoza, Argentina; Paso Robles, Russian River Valley, and Carneros, California; Northern Rhône Valley, France; Columbia Valley and Walla Walla, Washington
Varietals: Chardonnay, Grenache Blanc, Marsanne, Roussanne, Viognier
Technique: Full malolactic fermentation; oak aging, often in a mix of old and new wood, or just new wood
Characteristics: Reminiscent of eggnog in body, creaminess, and the presence of warm, baking spice influence
Color: Deep golden hues
Ideal Pairings: Thanksgiving flavors; stuffed mushrooms; pork chops with herbs and apples; Fall bisque soups; loaded nachos

9W

Climate: Warm, even hot, climates with beautiful sunshine and long stretches of ideal farming weather; almost all New World
Regions: Hawkes Bay, New Zealand; Napa Valley, Sonoma Valley, and Santa Lucia Highlands, California; Casablanca Valley, Chile; Malgas and Stellenbosch, South Africa
Varietals: Chardonnay, Chenin Blanc, Gewürztraminer
Technique: Primarily full ML and new-oak aging
Characteristics: Creamy and smooth with a lift of acid to avoid being boring
Color: Pale amber with golden tones
Ideal Pairings: BLTs; foie gras; bacon turkey burgers; sole meunière; lobster pizza

10W

Climate: New World (primarily American) climates with hot days and abundant sunshine and easy growing conditions
Regions: Napa Valley and Santa Maria Valley, California
Varietals: Chardonnay, Viognier
Techniques: Barrel fermentation and new-oak aging, with a preference for American oak
Characteristics: Rich and flavorful full-bodied wines with a voluptuous, creamy texture and a mouthfeel of heavy cream
Color: Warm, amber tones
Ideal Pairings: Mac & cheese; Fettuccine Alfredo; cream-based soups like corn or clam chowder; fried food; lobster; butter sauces

THE REDS

1R

Climate: Cool climates, some with alpine influence

Regions: Willamette Valley, Oregon; Burgundy, Beaujolais, and Jura, France

Varietals: Pinot Noir, Gamay, and Trousseau

Technique: Minimal maceration, often partially carbonic; primarily short periods of stainless-steel aging

Characteristics: Light-bodied with a mouthfeel of skim milk; bright, lip-smacking acidity

Color: Transparent, ruby red

Ideal Pairings: Thanksgiving flavors; salty charcuterie; seared fish; light salads; soft and fresh cheeses; Chinese take-out

2R

Climate: Cool climates with some maritime and alpine influence

Regions: Central Otago, New Zealand; Sonoma Coast, California; Burgundy and Loire Valley, France; Willamette Valley, Oregon; Piedmont, Italy

Varietals: Pinot Noir, Gamay, Barbera, Dolcetto

Technique: Short maceration; primarily steel or cement egg fermentation with limited oak aging

Characteristics: Light-bodied and lean with a mouthfeel resembling skim milk; tart and acidic.

Color: Transparent, ruby red with some purple highlights

Ideal Pairings: Tomatoes; savory herbs; mushrooms; red fruits; salmon; beef carpaccio; Thanksgiving flavors

3R

Climate: Temperate warmth, but some regions see more sun than others

Regions: Burgundy, France; Willamette Valley, Oregon; Anderson Valley and Russian River Valley, California; Etna and Piedmont, Italy; Long Island, New York

Varietals: Pinot Noir, Nerello Mascalese, Barbera, Cabernet Franc

Technique: A variety of techniques; cooler regions use mix of longer maceration, some barrel fermentation and aging; warmer climates use cement or stainless-steel aging and less oak

Characteristics: Light- to medium-bodied with a mouthfeel resembling 1% milk; juicy with ripe fruit and vibrant acidity

Color: Semi-transparent; ruby red to brick in color

Ideal Pairings: Grilled seafood; capers and olives; tomatoes and tomato sauces; pizza; salmon and tuna; salty/fatty appetizers; earthy vegetables

4R

Climate: A mix of cool and temperate climates, some with maritime and alpine influences

Regions: Sicily and Piedmont, Italy; Carneros and Russian River Valley, California; Bordeaux, Loire Valley, and Rhône Valley, France

Varietals: Nerello Mascalese, Nerello Cappuccio, Nebbiolo, Cabernet Franc, Sangiovese, and Grenache

Technique: A mix of steel and oak aging, and varying lengths of maceration

Characteristics: Mouthfeel resembling 2% milk; ripe fruit, balanced acid, and subtle tannins

Color: Semi-opaque red with purple and garnet tones

Ideal Pairings: Cured meats and sausages; grilled vegetables; steak salads; chicken dishes

5R

Climate: Temperate, mostly sunny climates; many with continued alpine or maritime influence

Regions: Tuscany and Sicily, Italy; Rhône Valley and Bordeaux, France; Shenandoah Valley, Virginia; Casablanca, Chile; Rioja, Spain

Varietals: Sangiovese, Nero D'Avola, Syrah, Cabernet Sauvignon, Merlot, Cabernet Franc, Carmenere, Tempranillo, Garnacha/Grenache

Technique: Longer maceration; oak aging, mostly done in used-oak barrels

Characteristics: Structured tannins and a medium body with a mouthfeel resembling whole milk; vibrant acidity; cellar worthy

Color: Semi-transparent core with ruby, purple, and garnet hues

Ideal Pairings: Braised meats; game meats; herbal flavors; earthy vegetables like eggplant and mushrooms; savory dishes

6R

Climate: Primarily warmer climates; a few cooler climate regions that see more manipulation

Regions: Piedmont and Tuscany, Italy; Rioja, Spain; Chateauneuf-du-Pape and St. Joseph, France; Douro Valley and Alentejo, Portugal

Varietals: Nebbiolo, Sangiovese, Tempranillo, Cabernet Sauvignon, Grenache, Syrah, Mourvèdre, Touriga Nacional, Aragonez

Technique: A variety of longer-period, oak-aging techniques; some regions blend wine to achieve desired result

Characteristics: Structured but balanced tannins; a mouthfeel of whole-milk-plus; palate-friendly and cellar-worthy

Color: Semi-opaque ruby, garnet, purple, and black tones

Ideal Pairings: Grilled meats; charred vegetables; wild boar; pasta and risotto; lobster

7R

Climate: Drier, warmer climates with more influence from the sun

Regions: Napa Valley and Sonoma County, California; Columbia Valley, Washington; Bandol, France; Ribera del Duero, Spain; Mendoza, Argentina; Puglia, Italy

Varietals: Zinfandel, Cabernet Sauvignon, Merlot, Syrah, Mourvèdre, Malbec, Negroamaro

Technique: Longer maceration; barrel fermentation; more frequent new-barrel-oak aging

Characteristics: Fuller bodied with a mouthfeel of half-and-half; palate-friendly, bold with ripe fruit and softer tannins

Color: Mostly opaque burgundy with garnet and plum tones

Ideal Pairings: Red meat; stews; herbs; Mediterranean flavors; Indian spices; high-acid foods

8R

Climate: Warm, sunny, and dry climates with long growing seasons

Regions: Priorat and Toro, Spain; Napa Valley and Sonoma County, California; McClaren Vale, Australia; Swartland, South Africa; Languedoc-Roussillon, France; Puglia, Italy

Varietals: Tempranillo, Cabernet Sauvignon, Zinfandel, Syrah/Shiraz, Grenache, Mourvèdre, Carignan, Negroamaro

Technique: Riper grapes; longer maceration; longer periods of aging, primarily in new-oak barrels

Characteristics: Abundant juice; overall smoother tannins with less acidity

Color: Opaque burgundy, with garnet and purple tones

Ideal Pairings: A wide variety of meat and potato dishes including steaks, lamb, meatloaf, and burgers; Asian flavors; chicken thighs; Brassica vegetables such as brussels sprouts, broccoli, and kale

9R

Climate: Warm to hot climates with arid conditions; mostly New World

Regions: Napa Valley and Dry Creek Valley, California; Walla Walla, Washington; Barossa Valley, Australia; Campania and Veneto, Italy; Mendoza, Argentina

Varietals: Cabernet Sauvignon, Petite Sirah, Zinfandel, Syrah/Shiraz; Aglianico; Corvina; Malbec

Technique: Harvest timed for optimal ripeness while maintaining acidity; long maceration; barrel fermentation and extended new-oak aging

Characteristics: Full-bodied wines that are juicy, jammy, and richly tannic

Color: Opaque with rich tones of burgundy, plum, and black

Ideal Pairings: Juicy, thick steaks and other red meat; barbecue; rich marinades; Osso Bucco; cream-based dishes; spicy foods

10R

Climate: Primarily the hottest and most arid growing regions

Regions: Walla Walla, Washington; Barossa Valley, Australia; Napa Valley and Paso Robles, California; Veneto, Italy

Varietals: Syrah/Shiraz, Petite Sirah, Zinfandel, Corvina

Technique: Very ripe fruit; new-oak fermentation and barrel aging; long periods of aging in barrel and bottle

Characteristics: Massive wines that are dense and flavorful with a mouthfeel of heavy cream; thick and jammy

Color: Opaque, rich burgundy, plum, and black colors

Ideal Pairings: Barbecue; balsamic reductions; richly flavored stews; umami flavors; rich, bold cheeses

INDEX

RECIPE INDEX

MORE GREAT BOOKS *from*
SPRING HOUSE PRESS

The Hot Chicken Cookbook
978-1-940611-19-8
$19.95 | 128 Pages

A Colander, Cake Stand, and My Grandfather's Iron Skillet
978-1-940611-36-5
$24.95 | 184 Pages

Secrets from the La Varenne Kitchen
978-1-940611-15-0
$17.95 | 136 Pages

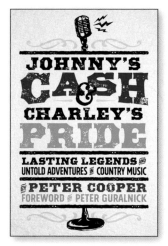

Johnny's Cash & Charley's Pride
978-1-940611-70-9
$17.95 | 260 Pages

SPRING HOUSE PRESS

Look for these Spring House Press titles at your favorite bookstore, specialty retailer, or visit *www.springhousepress.com.*
For more information about Spring House Press, call 717-208-3739 or email us at *info@springhousepress.com.*

MORE GREAT BOOKS *from*
SPRING HOUSE PRESS

The Cocktail Chronicles
978-1-940611-17-4
$24.95 | 200 Pages

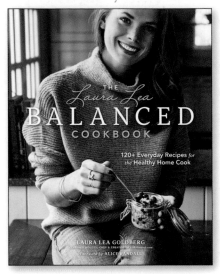

The Laura Lea Balanced Cookbook
978-1-940611-56-3
$30.00 | 368 Pages

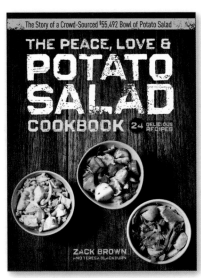

**The Peace, Love &
Potato Salad Cookbook**
978-1-940611-38-9
$16.95 | 80 Pages

The Natural Beauty Solution
978-1-940611-18-1
$19.95 | 128 Pages

SPRING HOUSE PRESS

Look for these Spring House Press titles at your favorite bookstore, specialty retailer, or visit *www.springhousepress.com*. For more information about Spring House Press, call 717-208-3739 or email us at *info@springhousepress.com*